THE HUNTING WIDOW'S GUIDE TO GREAT VENISON COOKING

VOL. 1: FAMILY FAVORITES

Copyright © 2010 Susan Rose

The Hunting Widow's Guide to Great Venison Cooking
Reston, VA 20190
www.greatvenisoncooking.com
ll rights reserved

The Hunting Widow's Guide to Great Venison Cooking: Volume 1—Family Favorites

Author: Susan Rose

Book Design: Karen Loehr

Photographers:
Peggy Tyree (cover and inside portraits)
Susan Rose (food)
Istockphoto.com (stock photos of deer)

Editors: Monica Parham, Susan Trivers

Proofreaders: Nina Seebeck, Dan Loehr

Printed by CreateSpace.

INTRODUCTION I ✪ THE SKINNY ON VENISON: NUTRITION FACTS 2 ✪ FARM TO FORK 5 ✪ BEFORE YOU COOK: TRIMMING 6 ✪ AGING MEAT 6 ✪ FREEZING MEAT 7 ✪ CANNING MEAT 7 ✪ GRINDING MEAT 7 ✪ COOKING TECHNIQUES USED IN THIS BOOK: GENERALCOOKING ADVISE 8 ✪ MARINATING 8 ✪ GRILLING 8 ✪ ROASTING 8 ✪ BROILING 9 ✪ PAN FRYING 9 ✪ BROWNING GROUND VENISON 9 ✪ BRAISING 9 ✪ STEWING 9 ✪ COOKING BURGERS 9 ✪ USING YOUR GAS GRILL AS A SMOKER 10 ✪ BUTTERFLYING MEAT 10 ✪ FRENCHING VENISON 10 ✪ MAKING VENISON STOCK 10 ✪ COOKING TECHNIQUES FOR NON-VENISON ITEMS IN THE BOOK 11 ✪ MAKING RECIPES GLUTEN FREE 12 ✪ ESSENTIAL COOKING TOOLS 11 ✪

Appetizers 14

HOT SEVEN-LAYER DIP 17 ✪ SAVORY SOUTHWESTERN VENISON PIE 17 ✪ VENISON CON QUESO 18 ✪ SOUTHWESTERN NACHOS 19 ✪ SMOKY VENISON QUESADILLAS 20 ✪ STEAK ON A STICK: TERIYAKI SKEWERS 21 ✪ TERIYAKI SAUCE 21 ✪ BBQ VENISON MEATBALLS 22 ✪ STUFFED MUSHROOM CAPS 22 ✪ PEPPER PINWHEELS 23 ✪ BERRY BACON PINWHEEL 24 ✪ PEPPER & VENISON CROSTINI 25 ✪ ASIAGO SANDWICHES 26 ✪ CHERRY DROPS 26 ✪ VENISON TENDERLOIN WITH BÉARNAISE SAUCE 27 ✪ BÉARNAISE SAUCE 27 ✪ BUFFALO VENISON TENDERS 28 ✪ BLUE CHEESE DRESSING 28 ✪ RILLETTES OF VENISON 29 ✪ COOKING THE NECK ROAST 29 ✪

Chili and Stew 30

VENISON CHIPOTLE CHILI 31 ✪ TWENTY MINUTE CHILI 32 ✪ CINCINNATI SKYLINE CHILI 33 ✪ WHITE VENISON CHILI 34 ✪ COFFEE CHILI 35 ✪ GUINNESS PUB STEW 36 ✪ TACO SOUP 37 ✪ FIESTA VENISON CHOWDER 37 ✪ FIG AND VENISON STEW 38 ✪ VENISON SHORBA SOUP 39 ✪ TUNISIAN VENISON TAGINE 40 ✪ VENISON AND WILD RICE SOUP 41 ✪ FAT TUESDAY JAMBALAYA 42 ✪

Casseroles and Comfort Food 43

VENISON LASAGNA 44 ✪ MOCK LASAGNA 45 ✪ VENISON STROGANOFF 46 ✪ VENISON AND ARTICHOKE ALFREDO 47 ✪ ENCHILADAS 48 ✪ CORN AND VENISON CASSEROLE 49 ✪ SPICY SOUTHWESTERN CASSEROLE 50 ✪ TRADITIONAL SHEPHERD'S PIE 51 ✪ UPSIDE DOWN SHEPHERD'S PIE 51 ✪ VAQUERO PIE 52 ✪ SCOTTISH MINCE PIE 53 ✪ THREE CHEESE PASTA AND VENISON 54 ✪ VENISON AND SMOKED GOUDA STRATA 55 ✪

CONTENTS

Burgers, Meatloaf, and Ground Meat 56

GOOD OLD AMERICAN BURGER 57 ❂ BBQ VENISON BURGER 57 ❂ CLASSIC BLUE BURGER 58 ❂ SPICY BURGERS 58 ❂ HUSH BURGERS 59 ❂ OAT BURGERS 60 ❂ HORSERADISH BURGERS 60 ❂ IRISH STYLE MEAT LOAF 61 ❂ GOOD OLD AMERICAN MEAT LOAF 61 ❂ APPALACHIAN MEAT LOAF 62 ❂ MEXICALI MEAT LOAF 62 ❂ TWICE-BAKED POTATOES 63 ❂ YUMMY-IN-THE-TUMMY VENISON POT PIE 64 ❂ VENISON CALZONE 64 ❂ VENISON MEAT SAUCE 65 ❂ NURENBURG STYLE BRATS 66 ❂ ANDOUILLE SAUSAGE 66 ❂ FLAVORFUL VENISON BREAKFAST SAUSAGE 67 ❂

Roasts, Steaks, and Entrées 68

SALT ROAST 69 ❂ SIMPLE OVEN ROAST 70 ❂ GARLIC AND HERB ROAST 71 ❂ APPLE ROTISSERIE ROAST 72 ❂ CHIPOTLE VENISON ROAST 73 ❂ VENISON SLOW COOKER POT ROAST 73 ❂ REINDEER WITH LINGONBERRY SAUCE 74 ❂ CORNED VENISON 75 ❂ GIGOT DE VENAISON 76 ❂ TRADITIONAL YANKEE POT ROAST 77 ❂ ROTISSERIE ROAST WITH GARLIC RUB 77 ❂ NUTTY VENISON SADDLE IN BACON 78 ❂ GRILLED TENDERLOIN MEDALLIONS 79 ❂ LOIN CHOPS WITH CRANBERRY ORANGE RELISH 80 ❂ LIMEY BEER STEAK 81 ❂ SAGE STEAK 81 ❂ SAVORY KABOBS 82 ❂ EASY CITRUS KABOBS 82 ❂ SOUTHWEST KABOBS 83 ❂ CILANTRO-LIME MARINADE 83 ❂ SCRUMPTIOUS CHOPS 84 ❂ RACK OF VENISON WITH SHALLOTS AND GARLIC 85 ❂ SAFFRON RACK 85 ❂ JALAPENO STUFFED TENDERLOIN 86 ❂ VENISON POTATO ROLL 87 ❂ MASHED RED POTATOES 87 ❂ SMOKED BBQ VENISON 88 ❂ JAEGER SCHNITZEL 89 ❂ TAQUERIA STYLE VENISON TACOS 90 ❂ ONION RELISH 91 ❂ ROASTED VEGETABLE SALSA 91 ❂ VENISON FAJITAS 92 ❂

Sandwiches and Salads 94

VENISON REUBEN SANDWICH 95 ❂ HOMEMADE THOUSAND ISLAND DRESSING 95 ❂ ROAST VENISON SANDWICH 96 ❂ AVOCADO AND ROAST SANDWICH 96 ❂ VENISON AND ARTICHOKE SALAD SANDWICH 96 ❂ VENISON SPINACH ADN PASTA SALAD 97 ❂ ROTINI WITH BASIL, TOMATO, AND VENISON 97 ❂ VENISON AND WILD RICE SALAD 98 ❂ STEAK SALAD WITH CRANBERRY DRESSING 99 ❂ CRANBERRY DRESSING 99 ❂ ARUGULA AND BLUE CHEESE SALAD WITH VENISON 100 ❂ GRILLED VENISON SALAD WITH TANGY LEMON DRESSING 100 ❂ TANGY LEMON DRESSING 100 ❂ SPINACH SALAD WITH GRILLED VENISON TENDERLOIN 101 ❂ BALSAMIC VINAIGRETTE 101 ❂ MEXICAN CHEF SALAD 102 ❂ MEXICAN THOUSAND ISLAND DRESSING 102 ❂ SOUTHWEST VENISON SALAD 103 ❂ CHIPOTLE RANCH SALAD 103 ❂ VENISON CHEF SALAD 103 ❂

For the Hunter: Harvesting Meat 105

THE CHALLENGES OF HARVESTING VENISON 106 ❂ HOW TO PROPERLY HARVEST DEER 106 ❂ FIELD DRESSING THE DEER 106 ❂

ACKNOWLEDGEMENTS 110 ❂ RESOURCES 110 ❂

Index 111

When I was a little girl dreaming about my future husband, I imagined someone smart, kind, funny, and handsome. He would be handy around the house, be a good cook, clean up after himself, put the toilet seat down, laugh at my jokes, and like my family. That was all that mattered.

A few years ago I found a man who is all those things...and more. He is a true Renaissance man; he not only cooks, he takes his bow out in the woods and hunts for our food. Then he brings it home and butchers it himself.

I'll be honest—I never dreamed I'd marry a hunter. For generations, the men in my family have done their hunting at the supermarket, very happy to be several steps removed from the origins of their food. Before I met Rick, I'd had venison twice. Once was in a fine French restaurant, where it was roasted to pink perfection. The other time was the experience most people have: a hunter gave a friend some steaks with no explanation of what to do with them. So we grilled them as we would beef, not knowing that they would cook twice as fast. The result was gamey, tough leather. Not delicious.

The first season Rick hunted, he brought home two small deer. I spent that winter learning what not to do with venison. The burgers and chili were good; the roasts and steaks were not.

The second season, we had four deer by November and Rick purchased a 7-cubic-foot freezer. I realized that if I didn't want to spend the year eating chili and burgers, I needed to learn how to cook venison. I wanted gourmet meals—roasts, tenderloins, kabobs, and other delicious favorites. I was willing to ruin some meat on the quest to learn what to do with venison.

I decided to chronicle my venison adventures in a blog, which then turned into a website: greatvenisoncooking.com. I experimented, and when something worked, I shared it. Over the course of the last few years, I have learned how to cook venison so that even the pickiest eaters enjoy it.

At this point, I've made hundreds of venison dishes. But for my first volume of the cookbook, I decided to go with the crowd-pleasers that everyone loves. These recipes are the ones I pull out for family gatherings, parties, and everyday eating. I hope you enjoy them as much as my family and friends do.

Here's a fun little history lesson: technically, the term venison describes the meat of any mammal killed by hunting. Throughout history, it applied to any animal from the families Cervidae (deer), Leporidae (hares), and Suidae (wild pigs), and certain species of the genus Capra (goats and antelopes). These days, if someone says they're serving venison, though, they're most likely talking about the meat from different species of deer.

Before I married a hunter, I didn't know there were different species of deer. But there are, and the species of deer you're likely to eat will depend on where you live and/or where the hunter in your life hunts. Whether White Tail or Mule, venison meat is typically richer and leaner than beef, the texture supple and tender. Depending on the diet of the deer, the flavor of the meat will vary slightly. Typically, it has a full, deep woody/berry taste (deer love, love, love fruit and berries). The biggest difference I find among the types of deer in terms of eating is that the farther west you go, the bigger the deer get. A bigger deer can be a tougher deer, so you need to keep that in mind when prepping the meat. If you're eating a big Wyoming buck, you may need to do some extra tenderizing.

Venison is most abundant in the winter because the traditional hunting season is October through December, beginning with the rut (when the bucks vie for the affection of does, which seem to love watching a good brawl) and ending when mating season is over. In areas like Northern Virginia, where the herds are seriously overpopulated, the regular season runs from September to March, with many bow hunters able to hunt year-round on damage-control permits.

If you're buying your venison in a store, or eating it in a restaurant, you're eating farm-raised meat. Generally, you need to go to a specialty butcher or high-end market to find it, and it's very expensive—we found venison tenderloin at our local butcher for $27 per pound. The venison you get in stores is very likely from New Zealand, although our butcher gets his from Pennsylvania. You can even order it on-line (page 110)—you gotta love the Internet! So even though the best bet for getting North American venison is to hunt, there are options if you really need your venison fix between hunting seasons.

NUTRITION FACTS

Venison is a great choice for people who love red meat, but who need to watch their cholesterol. It is an excellent protein source, but unlike beef, lamb, or pork, it tends to be low fat. For example, one serving of venison loin has 86% protein, 14% fat, 0% carbohydrates, and is only 81 calories. Not bad!

Figure 1 lists the nutritional composition of venison (source USDA). Many wonderful sources provided by healthcare professionals can tell you about the benefits of the various vitamins and minerals, so suffice it to say here that venison is really good for you. But the key takeaways are:

- Venison is low in saturated fats (2% of the Daily Value). In every serving of meat, there are 81 calories and only 12 are from fat.
- Venison is a very good source of vitamin B12 (60% of the Daily Value), as well as good or very good amounts of several other of the B vitamins, including riboflavin (40%), niacin (38%), and vitamin B6 (21.5%).

Figure 1

GAME MEAT, DEER, LOIN, SEPARABLE LEAN ONLY, 1" STEAK, COOKED, BROILED; 1 SERVING = 3OZ/85G

Nutrient	Units	1 serving	Nutrient	Units	1 serving
Proximates			Carotene, beta	mcg	0.0
Water	g	57.01	Carotene, alpha	mcg	0.0
Energy	kcal	128.0	Cryptoxanthin, beta	mcg	0.0
Protein	g	25.67	Vitamin A, IU	IU	0.0
Total lipid (fat)	g	2.02	Lycopene	mcg	0.0
Ash	g	1.06	Lutein + zeaxanthin	mcg	0.0
Carbohydrate, by difference	g	0.00	Vitamin E (alpha-tocopherol)	mg	0.53
Fiber, total dietary	g	0.0	Vitamin E, added	mg	0.00
Sugars, total	g	0.00	Vitamin K (phylloquinone)	mcg	1.0
Minerals			Fatty acids, total monounsaturated	g	0.298
Calcium, Ca	mg	5.0	Fatty acids, total polyunsaturated	g	0.088
Iron, Fe	mg	3.48	Cholesterol	mg	67.0
Magnesium, Mg	mg	26.0	**Amino acids**		
Phosphorus, P	mg	235.0	Tryptophan	g	0.229
Potassium, K	mg	338.0	Threonine	g	0.976
Sodium, Na	mg	48.0	Isoleucine	g	1.108
Zinc, Zn	mg	3.09	Leucine	g	1.964
Copper, Cu	mg	0.193	Lysine	g	2.097
Manganese, Mn	mg	0.025	Methionine	g	0.603
Selenium, Se	mcg	11.3	Cystine	g	0.241
Vitamins			Phenylalanine	g	0.976
Vitamin C, total ascorbic acid	mg	0.0	Tyrosine	g	0.807
Thiamin	mg	0.238	Valine	g	1.254
Riboflavin	mg	0.436	Arginine	g	1.543
Niacin	mg	9.143	Histidine	g	0.771
Pantothenic acid	mg	0.738	Alanine	g	1.506
Vitamin B-6	mg	0.643	Aspartic acid	g	2.241
Folate, total	mcg	8.0	Glutamic acid	g	3.663
Folic acid	mcg	0.0	Glycine	g	1.410
Folate, food	mcg	8.0	Proline	g	1.133
Folate, DFE	mcg_DFE	8.0	Serine	g	0.892
Choline, total	mg	96.0	Hydroxyproline	g	0.374
Betaine	mg	12.6	**Other**		
Vitamin B-12	mcg	1.56	Alcohol, ethyl	g	0.0
Vitamin B-12, added	mcg	0.00	Caffeine	mg	0.0
Vitamin A, RAE 0	mcg_RAE	0	Theobromine	mg	0.0
Retinol	mcg	0.0			

Source: http://www.nal.usda.gov/fnic/foodcomp/cgi-bin/list_nut_edit.pl

Figure 2

NUTRITIONAL COMPARISON OF MEATS

Meat	Calories (3 oz)	Fat (gm)	Cholesterol (gm)	Protein (gm)
Halibut, broiled	111	3	62	20
Turkey, white meat	133	3	59	26
Venison, leg cut	139	5	62	22
Chicken Breast, no skin	140	3	72	26
Salmon, broiled	140	5	60	21
Lamb Leg roast, lean	153	6	74	24
Veal Cutlet	155	4	112	28
Turkey, dark meat	159	6	72	24
Bass, broiled	167	3	62	18
Chicken Breast, with skin	167	7	72	25
Beef Tenderloin	174	8	72	24
Lamb, Loin Chop	183	8	80	25
Beef Bottom round, lean	189	8	81	27
Pork Shoulder, lean	207	13	82	22
Ground Beef, 85% lean	213	12	84	25
Pork, Top Loin	219	13	80	24
Beef Brisket	223	13	77	24
Ground Beef, 72% lean	248	18	77	20

Source: US Department of Agriculture and ESHA Research analysis of venison done
by The National Food Laboratory, Inc.

In fact, venison scores better in nutritional comparisons than chicken. Figure 2 shows the key nutritional values of venison versus other meats.

What should you make of this? You can eat venison every day. It's good for you.

FARM TO FORK

In my town in Northern Virginia, consumers have become interested in supporting local farmers. The grocery stores advertise the local produce—local seemingly defined as up to about 700 miles away. Farmers' markets and food co-ops are becoming more common. This is great. Buying locally is good for the local economy and good for the environment.

What's interesting is that I never hear talk of buying local meats. While there is plenty of locally raised meat on the market, it doesn't seem to be on the forefront of discussions about buying locally. We've got local butchers at our farm market, but I never see local meat at the grocery store.

What does this have to do with venison? Hunted venison is a locally grown, free-range food source. When I serve venison, I know where the animal lived, what it ate, and how old it was. I love that. I don't get that kind of information when I buy chicken or beef. I think being connected to our food sources is a good thing—it makes us more appreciative of the bounty we have. And, it's better for you. I like knowing the meat I eat is free from manufactured hormones.

If prepared and cooked well, venison is heavenly. If prepared poorly, it's disgusting. There is no middle ground. I'm willing to bet if you generally like red meat, but hate venison, it's because you've been the victim of sloppy prep work and overcooking. I know from experience how easy it is to ruin an excellent cut of venison meat, so I have assembled some guidelines on how to prepare and cook it so that it is delicious every time. The following are some guidelines on preparing and storing the meat.

TRIMMING

This is the most important step for roasts, medallions, or steaks. Always, always trim off as much fat, silverskin (the pearlescent membrane), or connective tissue (fascia) as possible. This task can be a bit of a pain, but it is critical to reducing the gamey taste. My rule is if I can't trim the fascia, it goes in the grinder for burgers or sausages (which camouflage the gamey taste better). What is the fascia? It's an uninterrupted, three-dimensional web of tissue that extends from head to toe, from front to back, from interior to exterior. It is very thin and filmy, and is often not removed during butchering at the processing center (because it's a pain to remove it). You can generally put the tip of the knife under it and pull it back off the meat. It's not hard, it's just tedious.

AGING MEAT

How old the deer was will impact the taste of the meat, and determine whether you need to age it, which improves the tenderness and flavor. If you've got a one-year-old animal, you can eat it immediately; it doesn't need to age at all—think spring lamb or veal. You can do anything you want with this meat! The older animals, like the 10-point trophy buck, are tough. They need to go through an aging process in order to make good eating. There is some debate over how long you need to age your venison. I find it really depends on how big and old the animal was.

Most hunters age their meat by hanging the carcass in the garage or a shed and letting it sit. While the U.S. Department of Agriculture wouldn't approve of this, it works if the temperatures are cold enough. When aging, you must keep the meat between 32°F and 40°F and keep it dry—bacteria will grow if the meat is warmer than 40°F and has any moisture in it.

We don't have any place to age meat, which is fine since we actually rarely do it. However, if Rick gets a buck that needs some aging, he quarters the deer and puts the meat in coolers with dry ice for a few days, which is sufficient for the does. For the bucks, we borrow our friend Bob's aging refrigerator and let the meat sit there for a week or so.

FREEZING MEAT

We freeze our meat to store it. Before we freeze the meat, we trim it as best we can. Whether you trim before or after you freeze is really up to you; I do it before freezing because I don't want to deal with that when I'm getting ready to cook.

We use wax-coated butcher paper to wrap the meat, then label it with the cut of meat and date. Our goal is never to let the meat sit in the freezer more than six months, so freezer burn is not an issue. If you're going to keep it for up to a year, vacuum-sealed bags work well.

We prefer to thaw the meat in the refrigerator, which can take a few days for a large roast. If you need to defrost it in the microwave, do so very slowly because you don't want to cook the meat during the defrosting stage. We usually defrost for 5 minutes at power setting 1, let it sit for 15 minutes, turn it over, and do it again. This takes time, but is worthwhile. Depending on how quickly you got it in the freezer to begin with, the meat will last up to three days after thawing.

CANNING MEAT

Canning is another great—and popular—way to store the meat. Since the subject is worthy of its own cookbook, and since I've never actually done it myself, I won't go into detail here. There are great resources on the Internet that provide detailed instructions and recipes for canned venison.

GRINDING MEAT

You can grind any of the meat, but typically you'll want to save the loins, backstraps, and roasts for other uses. We save any scrap meat and grind that. I suggest grinding the meat as you prepare to eat it, rather than grinding then freezing, because ground meat can be more prone to freezer burn. (Although if you're going to eat it within a month or two, that's not really an issue.) Grinding slightly frozen meat is ideal; it will move through the grinder much more smoothly. After grinding, cook it within a day or two. We use a grinder attachment for our stand mixer, although an actual meat grinder would be even better.

Many of the recipes in this book call for preparing the meat, or another key ingredient, in a specific way.

GENERAL COOKING ADVICE

Both dry-heat and moist-heat cooking methods work well for venison. Dry heat includes grilling, roasting, broiling, and pan frying. Moist heat includes braising and stewing. Dry heat is best for the high-quality loins, backstraps, and rump—they make the best kabobs, steaks, and medallions. Moist heat is best for the lesser-quality cuts, which make great stews, slow-cook roasts, and meat loaf.

I've found that for dry-heat cooking, you want to cook the meat for much shorter times; you'll want the meat rare to medium rare. For moist-heat cooking, you want to cook the heck out of the meat…like keeping the roast in the juices for 12 hours until it's toughened up then gotten tender again. Actual cooking times will depend on your oven or grill. Venison typically cooks much faster than beef. A good rule of thumb is hot-n-fast or low-n-slow, depending on the cut. The recipes here include cooking times for a general reference, but you may need to adjust them for your grill or oven.

Well Done or Rare? Because venison is so low in fat and doesn't have much juice, it is best rare. It doesn't take much to move from rare to leather with venison, so you need to watch it carefully while cooking. A good meat thermometer is an essential tool. Of course there are many hunters who won't eat venison if it's not well done, so for them I recommend moist-heat cooking and/or serving the venison with a good sauce.

MARINATING

Good for mature meat. Marinating venison is great for flavoring the meat, but it serves a practical purpose too. If you know you have a gamey piece of meat (for example, it came from a mature buck), marinating it can get rid of some of that gamey taste. Rinsing and marinating the meat in vinegar (apple cider, wine, whatever you like) for a few hours or marinating it in buttermilk overnight are especially effective techniques. Don't marinate it longer than 24 hours, though, because the meat will get mushy. If I'm making skewers or kabobs, I marinate the meat anywhere from 30 minutes to 2 hours, no more.

GRILLING

Good for tenderloin, backstraps, rump cuts, and burgers. Grill to medium rare to medium. The meat will cook very quickly—at least half the time it takes for a comparable cut of beef. So don't take your eyes off it until you get a feel for how quickly your grill cooks.

ROASTING

Good for tenderloin, leg, or rump roast. Trim it well before roasting. We usually roast it in an uncovered pan at 200° for about 20 to 25 minutes per pound. Since the venison will cook faster than beef, use a meat thermometer (your meat thermometer is your best friend when cooking venison).

Take the roast out when it's 5 to 10 degrees under what you're aiming for. Let it sit for 10 minutes or so, until it reaches the temperature you want. Here is an internal temperature chart:

Rare: 130° to 135°
Medium Rare: 135° to 140°
Medium: 140° to 145°
Medium Well: 150° to 155°
Well Done: 155° to 160°

BROILING

Good for tenderloins, backstraps, steaks, or chops. Preheat broiler and trim the meat. Cook 4 to 7 minutes per side, depending how thick the cut is. You want it browned, but not charred. You also want to pull it out before it's completely done and let it sit for a few minutes until it reaches the internal temperature you want.

PAN FRYING

Good for tenderloins, backstraps, steaks, or chops. Heat a heavy frying pan and add bacon fat, butter, or oil (depending on the recipe). Cook the venison quickly over high heat. Wait until the blood rises to the top, then flip it and wait for the same to happen on the other side (cooking time varies with thickness).

BROWNING GROUND VENISON

Because venison is so lean, it doesn't produce the fat that beef does when you brown the ground meat. So, to brown ground venison for chili, stew, or any other recipe that requires cooking the ground meat first, I use one tablespoon of canola oil per pound of meat. Heat the oil in a skillet, then add the venison. Stir until meat is cooked through. If there is any excess oil in the pan, drain it off. However, that is very rare!

BRAISING

Good for less tender cuts of meat like a chuck, round, neck, or shoulder roast. For braising venison, the trick is to cook it past the point where it gets tough. We typically braise roasts for 10 to 12 hours.

STEWING

Good for less tender cuts like the shank or neck meat. Cut the meat into 1- or 2-inch cubes. I tend to add my stew meat at the end of the cooking process so that it stays tender when we eat it.

COOKING BURGERS

Venison burgers may fall apart on the grill if you aren't careful about how you put them on (even if you've added a binding agent, like fat or breadcrumbs, to them). We use a huge grill spatula and gently transfer the raw meat to the grill. Make sure you spray the grill with non-stick spray; that will help. We've also found that if the meat is chilled the burgers are less likely to fall apart.

USING YOUR GAS GRILL AS A SMOKER

If you don't have a smoker, don't worry—your grill will work just fine. You'll need a gas grill with two or more individually controlled burners under the grate, plus a temperature gauge. If your grill doesn't have one, pick one up at any store that sells grill parts; it's important that you know what the temperature is inside the grill. Ideally, your grill will be able to maintain a constant temperature of 225°.

Turn on the left or back burner and heat the grill to 225°. Place foil-wrapped smoking wood over the heated burner. Put the meat on the unlit burner: the key to smoking is indirect heat. Smoke until meat is cooked through. Sausages take about 1 hour; a roast takes about 3 hours.

BUTTERFLYING MEAT

Butterflying is a way to make a steak thinner, which is ideal for stuffing or rolling meats. Flank steaks and backstraps work best. Lay the meat on a cutting board with the long side facing you. Begin to slice the steak in half horizontally, making sure you're keeping the halves even. Don't "saw" the meat with the knife, but rather slash in short strokes, pulling the top part back to reveal the inside of the steak. If you find yourself sawing, stop and sharpen your knife. Slice carefully so the meat stays intact; you want it to remain in one piece. Stop cutting when the meat gets to a point that it can lay flat when opened. At that point, you can use it as-is or pound it thinner between two sheets of plastic wrap or wax paper using a tenderizer. Be careful if you're pounding it—venison tears very easily.

FRENCHING VENISON

"Frenching" refers to a specific way to cut food. For meat, it means that a portion of the meat has been separated from the bone, such as a chop or a rib, by cutting the meat from the end of the bone. When you see ribs with the end of the bones sticking out, that's Frenched meat. It's done to help the meat cook evenly, and it looks nice on the plate.

MAKING VENISON STOCK

So many recipes call for stock or broth. You can certainly use beef or chicken stock, but venison stock is easy to make and it freezes well. Making venison stock is very similar to making beef stock, so if you have a recipe you like for that just use it. Otherwise, try this one. One note: these measurements are really a helpful guide. I've made it with only 1 pound of bones when that's all I've had. I've also thrown chicken bones in just because I had them. This recipe yields about 1 gallon of stock.

Ingredients*

5 pounds venison bones (preferably marrow bones)

2 pounds scrap meat (anything you would have otherwise thrown out)

2 onions chopped in half (or scrap pieces of onion from dinner)

2 medium carrots, diced

2 large ribs of celery, diced

Water (enough to cover the bones by about 1 inch)

2 bay leaves

Directions

Preheat oven to 400°.

Put bones in roasting pan and roast until well browned, about 40 minutes.

Put bones, meat, vegetables, and bay leaves in a pot large enough to hold everything.

Add water, covering everything by about 1 inch.

Bring to a gentle boil then cover and reduce heat to a very slow simmer for at least 6 hours, skimming occasionally.

Uncover and simmer for 2 more hours.

Strain and discard the solids.

Cool, uncovered, on the counter (don't cover it or it may sour).

When fully cooled, cover and store. I store in 2-cup freezer-safe bowls and freeze it.

*These ingredients are a guideline only. Use more or less of anything depending on what you have on-hand. I usually save onions, carrots, and celery pieces that I haven't used and throw them into the stock.

COOKING TECHNIQUES FOR NON-VENISON ITEMS IN THE BOOK
Butter: Salted or Unsalted

Many of the recipes call for butter. I use unsalted butter for all of my cooking; I'd rather control how salty the food tastes. However, you can use whatever type of butter you have on hand. Just remember that these recipes assume the butter is unsalted.

I also prefer real butter to margarine because it melts better, and tastes better. If I want to be healthier, I'll use cooking oil as a substitute rather than margarine.

Roasting Peppers

There are several ways to roast peppers. I'm a fan of easy, so I put the whole peppers on a baking sheet under the broiler. After a few minutes, when the top has charred, flip them to the other side. Do that until all sides are charred. How long it takes will depend on the size of the peppers.

When charred, remove the peppers from the oven and set aside. Some people put them in brown paper bags to cool, but if you don't have one, don't worry. I just set them aside to cool. Once cool, run them under cold water to peel off the skin. Then slice them according to the recipe.

MAKING RECIPES GLUTEN FREE

I have a good friend with a serious gluten allergy, so I've learned how to make my recipes gluten free. It's really very easy, and I often find I prefer the gluten-free version. Try the following gluten-free substitutions:

Flour	Almond Meal
Bread Crumbs	Crushed Oats
	Almond Meal
Wheat Pasta	Gluten-free Pasta

ESSENTIAL COOKING TOOLS

In general, I believe simple is better in the kitchen. That's why I pretty much use one knife (an 8-inch chef's knife), one skillet, and one stock pan, regardless of what I'm making. But there are a few tools that I use when preparing venison that really make a difference, and will appear in many of the recipes in this book. If you don't have these items, maybe a little hint to your honey is in order.

Stand Mixer with Meat Grinder and Sausage Stuffer

The stand mixer is phenomenal for thoroughly mixing the ingredients I use for meat loaves and sausages. Sure, your hands will work. But the stand mixer with the hook attachment is better.

I also use the stand mixer with the meat grinder attachment to grind meat. It's so much faster than a hand grinder; we've ground an entire doe in a few hours. I also use it for stuffing sausages. The attachments work very well.

Rotisserie Grill Attachment

Our gas grill has an electric rotisserie attachment, which is a great way to cook roasts on the grill. The rotisserie ensures the meat is cooked evenly all the way through. And, of course, we use it for chicken and duck, too.

Mortar and Pestle

I've had several mortars in my cooking career, some that work better than others. These days I have two, both of heavy stone. One holds one cup and I use it only for crushing spices. The other holds four cups, and I use it for meat, guacamole, and other wet foods. Both cost less than $25 each, never slip on the counter, and make beautiful decorations when not in use. Rick got the small one at a local Indian food mart and ordered the larger one online.

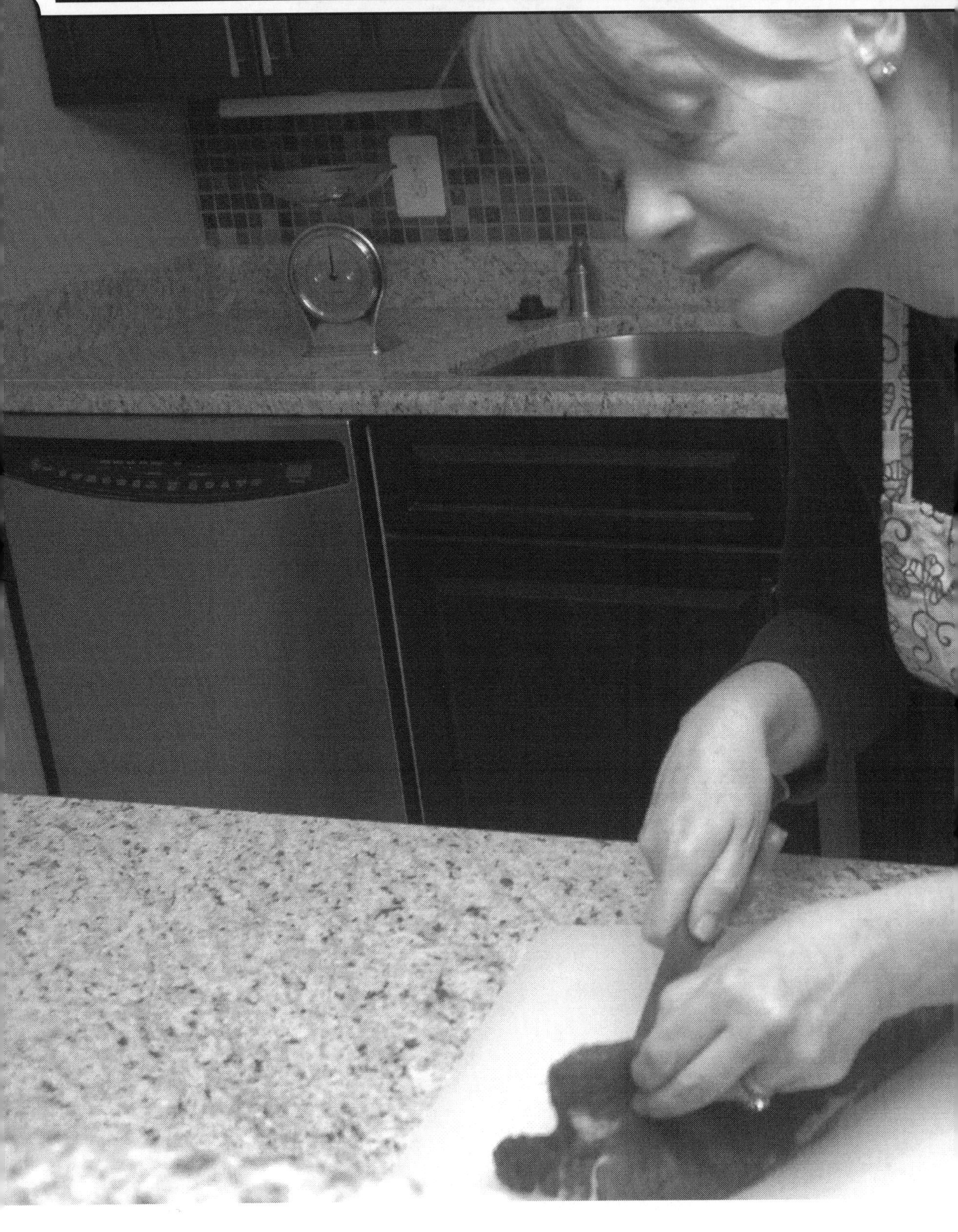

Whether you're making a sit-at-the-table-with-the-whole-family dinner or you need a tasty appetizer for game day, you'll find what you need in these pages. Every recipe in this volume has been tested on the pickiest of eaters, and all have gotten the thumbs up.
Enjoy!

The practice of serving tiny little morsels of yumminess before the main meal dates back to 300 BC in Greece. The Greeks' appetizers usually consisted of garlic and sea urchins. The Romans adopted that idea and did what they did with everything—took it to its extreme. A Roman appetizer buffet, the course before the banquet main course, but after the "appetite stimulation course," included eggs, casseroles, sausages, cheese, and other hearty dishes. I say the Romans were on to something.

Hot Seven-Layer Dip

SERVES 8

Ingredients	Directions
½ (12-ounce) can refried beans	Preheat oven to 350°.
1 (12-ounce) jar salsa (mild or spicy)	Spread the beans on the bottom of an 8 by
¼ pound ground venison, browned (page 9)	8-inch baking dish. Mix about ½ cup salsa with
2 cups grated Cheddar cheese	the venison. Spread over the beans. Spread the
1 jalapeño pepper*, cored, seeded, and sliced	cheese over the meat. Layer the jalapeño slices over the cheese.
1 cup guacamole	
8 ounces sour cream	Bake until cheese melts, about 15 to 20
10 black olives, sliced	minutes. Remove from oven.
	Layer on the remaining salsa, guacamole, and
You can use canned jalapeño peppers if you can't find a fresh one.	sour cream. Sprinkle the olives on top. Serve with tortilla chips.

Savory Southwestern Venison Pie

MAKES 1 PIE

Ingredients	Directions
2 cups tortilla chips, crushed	Preheat oven to 325°.
6 tablespoons butter, melted	In a medium bowl, combine tortilla chips and
2 (8-ounce) packages cream cheese, softened	butter. Press into bottom of a springform pan.
2 eggs	Bake 15 minutes, remove from oven, and leave oven on.
1 (4-ounce) can diced green chilies, drained	
1 fresh jalapeño pepper, cored, seeded, and diced	In a large bowl, blend cream cheese and eggs.
8 ounces Colby-Jack cheese, grated	Add green chilies, jalapeño, Colby-Jack, and
1 pound ground venison, browned (page 9)	venison. Pour over crust and bake 30 minutes
½ cup guacamole	(be careful not to overcook). Remove from oven and cool in the pan for 5 minutes.
2 plum tomatoes, diced	
	Run knife around inside edge and remove sides from pan. Spread guacamole over top and sprinkle with tomatoes. Serve with tortilla chips.

Venison Con Queso

SERVES 4 TO 10

Ingredients	Directions
½ pound ground venison	Brown the venison and the chili powder in 1 tablespoon of the oil. Set aside.
½ teaspoon chili powder	
2 tablespoons cooking oil	Roast the poblano and serrano peppers (page 12), then peel and remove the stems and seeds. Slice the peppers into ½-inch strips.
1 poblano chili pepper	
2 serrano peppers	
½ small onion, minced	Heat the remaining oil in a sauce pan. Add the onion and garlic and sauté until the onion is transparent. Add the peppers, cheese, and half and half, and then cook over low heat, stirring constantly, until the cheese is creamy, about 5 minutes. Add browned venison. Salt to taste.
2 cloves garlic, finely chopped	
2 cups shredded Monterey Jack cheese	
¾ cup half and half creamer	
Salt, to taste	
Corn chips or flour tortillas	Transfer to a slow-cooker dip bowl or heated chafing dish and serve immediately along with chips.

Southwestern Nachos

SERVES 2 TO 6

Ingredients	Directions
Cilantro-Lime Marinade (recipe page 83) **Nonstick cooking spray** **¾ pound venison steaks or kabob meat** **1 (15-ounce) can black beans, drained** **4 medium/large Roma tomatoes, diced** **8 tablespoons chopped scallions** **Blue corn tortilla chips** **Grated Cheddar cheese** **Sour cream** **Salsa** **Guacamole**	Lightly coat a grill with nonstick cooking spray and heat to 300°. Grill the venison until medium rare, about 3 minutes per side. Remove venison and slice into 1-inch strips. Mix together the venison, beans, tomatoes, scallions, and dressing. Spread tortilla chips on a microwave-safe plate. Spread venison mixture over chips and sprinkle with cheese. Microwave on high for 2 minutes (or until cheese is melted). Dollop sour cream, salsa, and guacamole over nachos.

Smoky Venison Quesadillas

SERVES 8 TO 16

Ingredients	Directions
1 cup barbecue sauce	Preheat grill to 350°.
2 cups shredded venison roast (page 29) or 2 cups chopped cooked venison steaks	Mix the barbecue sauce with the venison and set aside.
2 tablespoons butter	
8 flour tortillas	Butter one side of each tortilla, and place tortillas butter-side down on a plate. Cover half of each tortilla with venison, pico de gallo, and cheese. Fold the other half of the tortilla over the covered half. Place on the grill and cook for 1 to 2 minutes, until the tortilla starts to brown and crisp. Flip and continue grilling until other side is done. For a wonderful, smoky flavor, put the lid on the grill down while cooking to hold in the smoke.
1 cup pico de gallo	
1 to 2 cups Monterey Jack cheese, grated	
Sour cream	
Guacamole	
Picante sauce (fresh if you can find it)	

Remove from the grill and cut into 4 to 6 wedges (depending on how large you want the appetizer to be). Serve with sour cream, guacamole, and picante sauce.

You can make these on the stove if you can't get to the grill. Use a skillet on the medium-high setting.

Steak on a Stick: Teriyaki Skewers
SERVES 8

Ingredients	Directions
½ to 1 pound venison, cut into strips (about ½-inch wide by 3 to 5 inches long) Teriyaki sauce Bamboo skewers 1 cup sesame seeds	Cut the venison into strips and place in a container with a lid. Cover the meat with teriyaki sauce (recipe follows). If the sauce doesn't cover the meat, add water until all pieces are submerged. Marinate in refrigerator for ½ hour to 2 hours (the longer the meat marinates, the more tender it will be). After marinating, put meat on skewers, threading well enough so the meat won't fall off when cooking. Clean out the container and put the skewered meat back into it. Pour sesame seeds over the meat, cover, and shake so that the seeds coat all the meat. Preheat grill to 350°. Place the skewers on the grill. By the time you've put the last one down, it will be time to flip. They generally take 3 minutes to cook. These are best when cooked on the grill, but they work in the broiler too. Either way, watch them closely because they cook very fast, and if overcooked they taste like leather.

SIDE NOTE:
Because you are marinating this, you don't have to use prime cuts of meat. Just make sure you're using pieces of venison that you can cut into strips. The tougher the meat, the longer you want to marinate it. If you're using your trophy buck, marinate the skewers for 2 hours. If it's a small doe, ½ hour should do the trick.

Teriyaki Sauce

Ingredients	Directions
¼ cup soy sauce 1 cup water 1 tablespoon minced ginger (fresh or from a jar) 3 tablespoons brown sugar 1 clove garlic, minced ½ teaspoon honey 1/4 cup cold water (if needed to thin sauce)	Combine all the ingredients in a saucepan and bring to a boil, stirring constantly to allow the sauce to thicken. Once it reaches a boil, take it off the heat and let it cool. If it looks too thick, add the cold water until it's the consistency you want.

BBQ Venison Meatballs
SERVES 8

1 pound ground venison	Directions
¾ cup plain bread crumbs	
½ cup finely chopped parsley	Combine the venison, bread crumbs, parsley, salt, pepper, and eggs in a large bowl. Form into meatballs, using about 1 level tablespoon for each. (You can make them bigger if you want, but this is a nice appetizer size).
½ teaspoon salt	
¼ teaspoon freshly ground black pepper	
4 eggs, lightly beaten	
2 tablespoons olive oil	
2 jars BBQ sauce (enough to cover the meatballs in the slow cooker)	Heat the oil in a frying pan over medium-high heat. Add meatballs; cook on each side until browned so they won't fall apart in the slow cooker. As the meatballs are done, transfer them to your slow cooker. Cover with BBQ sauce and cook on low for 2 to 3 hours (until the meatballs are cooked through).

Stuffed Mushroom Caps
SERVES UP TO 18

Ingredients	Directions
½ pound ground venison	Preheat oven to 375°. Mix the venison, oil, and spices in a bowl. Set aside.
2 tablespoons olive oil	
¼ teaspoon ground allspice	
½ teaspoon garlic powder	Wash the mushrooms and pat dry with towel. Remove the mushroom stems by gently twisting and pulling. Place the mushroom caps in a baking dish and spoon the meat mixture into the caps. Put enough meat in each cap so that the meat peeks over the top.
½ tablespoon dried parsley	
Pepper	
Salt	
18 medium Crimini or white mushrooms	
	Bake for 15 to 20 minutes, until meat is cooked through. Serve immediately.

Pepper Pinwheels

SERVES 4

Ingredients	*Directions*
¼ cup cream cheese, room temperature 2 cloves garlic, pressed 1 tablespoon olive oil, plus extra to rub on the meat 2 roasted red peppers (fresh or jarred), chopped ½ pound venison flank steak, butterflied (instructions page 10) *Photo page 16*	Preheat oven or grill to 325°. Mix the cream cheese, garlic, oil, and peppers together well. I use a mortar and pestle to make sure they're really mixed. Spread the cream cheese mixture over the meat. Roll the meat gently, and tie off with cooking string. Rub meat well with olive oil. Pan sear over medium high heat on the stove top. Transfer to a baking dish if going in the oven, or put on the grill. Cook for about 10 minutes, turn and cook another 10 minutes, until meat is medium rare (135°) in middle (if you have a very thick piece of meat, you may need to cook longer). Let sit for about 10 minutes and slice into 1-inch-thick slices.

Berry Bacon Pinwheel

SERVES 4

Ingredients	*Directions*
¼ cup cream cheese	Preheat oven or grill to 325°.
3 strips apple smoked bacon, cooked crisp and crumbled	Mix the cream cheese, crumbled bacon, and cherries together well.
¼ cup frozen cherries, thawed and chopped	Spread the cream cheese mixture over the meat. Roll the meat gently. Wrap the raw bacon around the meat, which will help hold it together. Fasten bacon with toothpicks.
½ pound venison flank steak, butterflied (instructions page 10)	
3 or 4 slices apple smoked bacon, raw	

Pan sear over medium high heat on the stove top. Transfer to a baking dish if going in the oven, or put on the grill. Cook for about 10 minutes, turn and cook another 10 minutes, until meat is medium rare (135°) in middle (if you have a very thick piece of meat, you may need to cook longer).

Let sit for about 10 minutes and then slice into 1-inch-thick slices.

Pepper & Venison Crostini

SERVES 8

Ingredients	*Directions*
1 baguette or French bread	Prepare the roast the day before. We use the Simple Oven Roast on page 70. You want the meat rare for the crostinis.
2 tablespoons olive oil	
3 tablespoons chopped drained roasted red peppers from jar	In a small bowl, mix the red peppers, olives, thyme, and vinegar for the relish. Cover and refrigerate. (You can make this the day before to save time.)
3 tablespoons slivered pitted black olives (I like Kalamata)	
1 teaspoon fresh thyme leaves	
1 teaspoon red wine vinegar	
6 ounces mascarpone, cream cheese, or goat cheese	Prepare the crostini. Turn the oven on to broil. Slice the bread into ¼ inch, diagonal slices. Place the slices on a baking sheet and brush tops with olive oil. Broil until lightly toasted (about 2 minutes). Remove, flip over and brush other side. Broil until lightly toasted on that side. Remove and set aside.
Baby arugula	
16 very thin slices rare roast venison	

Once the crostini have cooled, spread a thin layer of cheese on each slice, saving some to dollop on the meat. Place one or two pieces of arugula on each. Fold roast beef slices to fit crostinis and place atop the arugula. Top each with a bit of the cheese and about ½ teaspoon of the pepper/olive relish.

Arrange crostini on platter and serve.

Asiago Sandwiches

MAKES 24

Ingredients | *Directions*

20 Kalamata olives, pitted and coarsely chopped

1 tablespoon rinsed, drained, and chopped capers

1 teaspoon freshly squeezed lemon juice

2 teaspoons olive oil

½ teaspoon anchovy paste (optional)

Fresh cracked black pepper

Asiago cheese slices, package of 12 slices

24 arugula leaves

24 very thin slices rare roast venison (recipe page 70)

Combine olives, capers, lemon juice, olive oil, anchovy paste, and pepper. Mix well and set aside. You can save the leftovers for up to two weeks.

Cut each slice of Asiago into four squares. Place one square of Asiago on the cutting board and layer with one leaf of arugula, one slice of venison, and ½ teaspoon of the olive mixture, then top with another square of Asiago.

Cherry Drops

SEVERS 12

Ingredients | *Directions*

6 ounces venison tenderloin, grilled and chopped into very small pieces

8 ounces cream cheese, room temperature

½ cup frozen cherries, chopped

24 won ton wrappers

Nonstick cooking spray

Preheat oven to 350°.
Mix the venison, cream cheese, and cherries in a bowl and set aside.

Spray a mini-muffin tin with cooking spray. Place one won ton wrapper in each muffin cup, making a little nest. Fill each cup with about 2 teaspoons of the meat mixture. Place in oven, uncovered, and bake for 18 to 20 minutes, or until edges of the cups are golden brown and filling is heated through.

Arrange on a platter and serve immediately.

Venison Tenderloin with Béarnaise Sauce
SERVES 8 TO 16

Ingredients	Directions
1 (16-inch-long) tenderloin (preferably from a small doe) 1 clove garlic 1 tablespoon olive oil ¼ teaspoon pepper Béarnaise Sauce	Marinate the tenderloin in garlic, oil, and pepper for about 30 minutes in the refrigerator. Grill or roast the tenderloin, preferably to rare/medium rare. Set aside and let cool while preparing the sauce (recipe follows). Slice the tenderloin into thin (¹/8 inch) slices. Top with dollop of Béarnaise Sauce.

Béarnaise Sauce

Ingredients	Directions
8 ounces unsalted butter 1 teaspoon peppercorns, crushed ¼ cup finely chopped shallots ¼ cup white wine 1 tablespoon fresh tarragon 1 bouillon cube 3 egg yolks Juice of 1 lemon Dash Worcestershire sauce Pinch of pepper, salt, and cayenne 1 teaspoon water	Melt butter and set aside. Keep it warm until it's time to add the eggs. Place the crushed peppercorns, shallots, wine, tarragon, and bullion into a small sauce pan. Bring to a boil. Lower the heat to medium. Combine this mixture in a mixing bowl with egg yolks, lemon, Worcestershire sauce, pepper, salt, cayenne, and water. Be careful to add the eggs slowly so that they don't scramble. Keep slowly whipping until sauce takes on a nice, creamy texture. Remove bowl from heat occasionally to keep the eggs from scrambling. Once you've achieved the creamy texture, remove from heat and fold in the butter, drop by drop, until it is all mixed together.

Buffalo Venison Tenders

SERVES 8 TO 12

Ingredients	Directions
12-ounce venison steak, cut into 2½-inch chunks	Marinate the venison in the hot sauce for ½ hour in the refrigerator.
½ cup Louisiana hot sauce	
Nonstick spray or parchment paper	Preheat oven to 350°. Coat a baking sheet with nonstick spray or line with parchment paper.
¼ cup all-purpose flour	
½ teaspoon garlic powder	In a Ziploc bag, mix flour, garlic powder, cayenne pepper, and salt. Transfer the venison to the bag and shake.
¼ teaspoon cayenne pepper	
¼ teaspoon salt	
2 egg whites	Combine egg whites with the water and beat. Place the egg mixture in a shallow dish or bowl. Dip venison in egg mixture, then roll it in the bread crumbs. Place venison on the baking sheet. Bake for about 6 minutes in the preheated oven. Turn pieces over and bake 5 minutes longer, or until meat is firm to the touch.
1 tablespoon water	
¾ cup bread crumbs	
Celery sticks	
1 tablespoon water	
Blue Cheese Dressing (recipe follows; to be made an hour in advance)	
	Serve with celery sticks and Blue Cheese Dressing.

Blue Cheese Dressing

Ingredients	Directions
¼ cup crumbled blue cheese	Combine all ingredients in a small bowl and mix thoroughly. Refrigerate for 1 hour before serving.
2 tablespoons buttermilk	
½ cup light sour cream	
¼ teaspoon freshly ground black pepper	

Rillettes of Venison
SERVES 6 TO 10

A rillette is like pâté, although without the organ meat. It's a great spread on crackers or toast. Rillettes are best if they are refrigerated for at least a day (or three) before eating.

Ingredients	Directions
½ cup sherry	Pour sherry into a small sauce pan and bring it to a boil. Let boil for 1 minute to cook off the alcohol.
½ pound venison neck roast meat (recipe follows)	
¼ cup butter	
½ cup sour cream	Chop meat finely, until it is about the size and consistency of canned tuna fish. Set meat aside.
½ teaspoon salt	
¼ teaspoon pepper	
	Soften the butter in the microwave (about 10 seconds on high). Mix the meat, sherry, butter, sour cream, salt, pepper, and the seasoning for whichever version you're making. Transfer to a small (16-ounce) casserole dish, cover with saran wrap, and refrigerate for 1 to 3 days.
VERSION 1—HERBED RILLETTES	
¼ cup finely chopped fresh parsley	
¼ cup finely chopped fresh tarragon	
VERSION 2—HUNTERS' FAVORITE RILLETTES	
¼ teaspoon nutmeg	Spread on bread or crackers.
1 tablespoon Worcestershire sauce	
¼ teaspoon freshly ground black pepper	

Cooking the Neck Roast

Ingredients	Directions
Venison neck roast	Place the neck roast in a slow cooker. Cover with broth, until the liquid covers the meat by about 1 inch. If you need additional liquid to cover the meat, use water. Add 5 drops of liquid smoke. (Don't forget to add this; the smoky flavor is what makes the rillettes great.) Cook for 8 to 12 hours, until the meat falls apart easily.
6 cups venison stock (page 11) or chicken broth	
Liquid smoke	

The first chili recipes—at least in the United States—appeared in West Texas in the late 18th century. The recipes were handed down by word of mouth to the cowboys out on the range. Chili was a great meal for them—most cowboys weren't known for their cooking. Adding wonderful spices to the meat was a good way to mask the taste of overcooked meat of questionable freshness. Chili has come a long way since then!

Stew has been around a little longer. The first known stew recipes are found in the oldest cookbook known, De Re Coquinaria (*On Cookery*), written in the 4th or 5th century AD. Now that's a food that has withstood the test of time!

Venison Chipotle Chili

SERVES 8

Ingredients

1 tablespoon oil

1 medium onion, chopped

2 cloves garlic, minced

1 medium red bell pepper, chopped

1 medium green bell pepper, chopped

1 tablespoon chili powder

2 teaspoons ground cumin

2 pounds ground venison, browned (page 9)

1 (28-ounce) can plum tomatoes with juice, chopped

1 to 2 tablespoons chopped canned chipotle peppers in adobo sauce

Salt and pepper to taste

Directions

In a large, heavy saucepan, heat oil over medium heat. Add onions, garlic, and bell peppers. Cook until tender (5 to 10 minutes). Add chili powder and cumin and cook, stirring frequently, for 2 minutes. Add the venison, tomatoes, and chipotle peppers. Heat to boiling. Add a little water if it looks thicker than you like. Decrease the heat and simmer uncovered for at least 20 minutes. Season with salt and pepper.

Note of Warning: The chipotle peppers can pack a punch, so if you're feeding people who prefer their chili mild, then only use 1 tablespoon of them.

Note:
All of the chili recipes here can be eaten immediately, but they're really better the next day (after the flavors have gotten to know each other a little better).

Twenty Minute Chili

SERVES 8

Ingredients	Directions
3 tablespoons olive oil	Heat skillet over medium-high heat. Add oil and onion. Cook until soft and slightly browned, about 5 minutes. Add garlic and cook 1 minute. Add venison and cook with the onion mixture until browned and almost cooked through. Add tomatoes and cook 3 minutes. Bring to a boil. Add wine and cook 1 to 2 minutes, until the alcohol is cooked out. Add broth, parsley, salt, pepper, and spices. Cook for 5 minutes.

Serve with grated cheese and sour cream (optional). |
2 large red onions, coarsely chopped	
6 cloves garlic, finely minced	
2 pounds venison, ground	
1 (28-ounce) can diced tomatoes	
⅔ cup dry red wine	
2 cups venison stock (page 11) or chicken broth	
¼ cup chopped Italian parsley	
¼ teaspoon salt	
Ground black pepper to taste	
4 teaspoons ground cumin	
1-½ tablespoons chili powder	
1-½ teaspoons ground oregano	

Cincinnati Skyline Chili

SERVES 8

Ingredients	Directions
2 pounds ground venison	Heat oil in a large (6-quart) sauce pan. Brown the meat in the oil. Add the remaining ingredients and simmer for 2 to 4 hours. Serve.
1 tablespoon oil	
1 large onion, chopped	
1 (16-ounce) can tomato sauce	How's that for easy?
1 (6-ounce) can tomato paste	
4 cups water	*"Ways" to eat Cincinnati Chili*
1-½ teaspoons cumin	2-way: add chili to egg noodles or spaghetti
½ teaspoon cinnamon	3-way: 2-way plus grated Cheddar
1 tablespoon chili powder	4-way: 3-way plus chopped onions
1 tablespoon salt	5-way: 4-way plus kidney beans
½ teaspoon freshly ground black pepper	
½ teaspoon cayenne pepper	
1-½ teaspoons allspice	
1 teaspoon nutmeg	
1 teaspoon paprika	
½ teaspoon oregano	
½ teaspoon ground cloves	
1 tablespoon cocoa powder	
3 bay leaves	
2 dashes Worcestershire sauce	

NOTE:

Like many great things, Cincinnati Skyline Chili was the product of a failure…the failing of a hot dog and Greek food stand of a Macedonian immigrant, Tom Athanas Kiradjieff, who came to Cincinnati in 1922. The mostly German residents didn't care for it. So Tom took the spices from a Greek stew, changed the meat to ground beef, and added "American" spices like chili powder to the mix, served it over spaghetti, and called it "Chili." The natives loved it. He also came up with the idea of selling his Chili in "ways," which is a fun way to customize your dish.

White Venison Chili

SERVES 8

Ingredients	*Directions*
1 pound venison stew meat, cut into cubes	Brown the venison cubes and set aside. Heat the oil in a large Dutch oven or stew pot over medium-low heat. Add the onion and slowly cook until tender. Mix in the garlic, jalapenos, green chili peppers, cumin, oregano, and cayenne pepper. Continue to cook and stir the mixture until tender, about 3 minutes. Mix in the broth, venison, white beans, and corn. Simmer 15 minutes, stirring occasionally. Remove from heat and slowly stir in the cheese until melted. Serve with a dollop of sour cream.
1 tablespoon oil	
1 onion, chopped	
3 cloves garlic, crushed	
4 ounces diced jalapeno peppers (canned or fresh)	
4 ounces chopped green chili peppers (canned or fresh)	
2 teaspoons ground cumin	
1 teaspoon dried oregano	
1 teaspoon ground cayenne pepper	
2 cups venison stock (page 11) or chicken broth	This is great with blue corn tortilla chips. And the kids say I have to warn every one that it's *really spicy*.
3 (15-ounce) cans white beans, drained	
2 cups frozen corn	
1 cup shredded Swiss cheese	
Sour cream	

Coffee Chili

SERVES 8

Ingredients

1 tablespoon olive oil

1-½ to 2 pounds ground venison (use 2 pounds if you aren't adding the beans)

1 onion, chopped

1 red bell pepper, chopped

1 green bell pepper, chopped

3 large cloves garlic, minced

2 tablespoons chili powder

1 teaspoon cumin

1 teaspoon coriander

1-½ teaspoons salt

½ teaspoon cinnamon

1 (28-ounce) can diced tomatoes, with juice

1 (6-ounce) can tomato paste

2 cups venison stock (page 11) or beef broth

1-½ cups brewed coffee (use a dark roast for more flavor)

1 tablespoon apple cider vinegar

1 (15-ounce) can beans (pinto, navy, or kidney), optional

Directions

Heat oil in a large Dutch oven or stew pot over medium heat. Add venison and stir to break up meat. When venison is almost cooked through, stir in the onion, peppers, garlic, chili powder, cumin, coriander, salt, and cinnamon. Cook until the vegetables soften slightly, about 5 minutes. Stir in beans (if you're adding them), tomatoes and the tomato paste. Then stir in broth, coffee, and vinegar. Increase heat and bring to a boil, reduce the heat, and simmer uncovered, stirring occasionally, until chili is as thick as you like. Let it simmer at least 1 hour.

Top it with grated Cheddar cheese, sour cream, chopped avocado, chopped jalapenos, or all of the above. Serve with tortilla chips.

Guinness Pub Stew

SERVES 12

Ingredients	Directions

3 tablespoons oil

3 pounds venison stew meat, cut into cubes

1 teaspoon salt

½ teaspoon freshly ground black pepper

3 large onions, chopped

6 large carrots, peeled, quartered lengthwise, and cut into 1-inch pieces

2 tablespoons minced garlic

36 ounces of Guinness (or another stout)

7 cups venison stock (page 11) or beef broth

2 bay leaves

3 tablespoons molasses

1 teaspoon Worcestershire sauce

2 tablespoons finely chopped fresh thyme

In a large Dutch oven or stew pot, heat the oil over medium-high heat. Season the venison with salt and pepper, then sear a couple of pieces of the meat to flavor the oil. Remove the seared meat and set aside (or give it to the dog for a nice little treat).

Reduce the heat to medium and add the onions. Use a wooden spoon to scrape the brown bits from the bottom of the pan. Cook for 10 minutes or until the onions begin to brown. Stir in the carrots and garlic, and cook for 5 minutes. Stir in the Guinness and enough stock to cover everything. Add the bay leaf, molasses, and Worcestershire sauce. Increase the heat to a boil, stir, and reduce to a simmer and cover. Simmer for 40 minutes or until the vegetables are fork tender. Add the venison and cook until meat is tender, 5 to 10 minutes. Add the fresh thyme, season to taste with salt and pepper, and serve.

IMPORTANT: If you can't find Guinness, use another stout. Do not use lager or any light beer—this just won't taste right.

Taco Soup

SERVES 8

Ingredients	Directions
1 medium onion, chopped	I make this in a slow cooker, but you could use the stove if you need to; just cook everything on low.
1 tablespoon oil	
1 package dry taco seasoning	
1 package dry ranch seasoning	Sauté the onions in oil over medium-high heat until they are tender.
2 (15-ounce) cans diced tomatoes, undrained	
1 (15-ounce) can diced tomatoes with green chilies, undrained	Put all the ingredients, except the venison, in the slow cooker and cook on low 4 to 6 hours.
1 (15-ounce) can black beans, drained	
1 (15-ounce) can pinto beans, drained	
1 ½ cups frozen whole kernel corn (or 1, 8-ounce, can of corn, drained)	Add the meat 20 to 30 minutes before you want to serve dinner. Cook until the meat is tender.
1 pound venison stew meat, cut into cubes	Serve with corn chips.

Fiesta Venison Chowder

SERVES 4 TO 8

Ingredients	Directions
1 to 2 pounds venison stew meat, cut into cubes (the amount depends on how much meat you like in your stews...we like a lot)	Put all ingredients except the cheese and chips into a slow cooker. Cook on low for 1 to 2 hours. Add the meat 20 to 30 minutes before serving. Serve in bowls and top with cheese and chips.
1 large red bell pepper, seeded and chopped	
2 cups frozen whole kernel corn	
1-½ cups milk (whole milk is best, but use what you like)	
1 can (11-ounce) cream of chicken or cream of corn soup	
1-½ cups mild salsa verde	
Juice of 2 limes	
1 can (15-ounce) beans with chilies	
1 cup grated Cheddar cheese	
Tortilla chips	

Fig and Venison Stew
SERVES 6 TO 8

Ingredients	Directions

9 ounces fresh figs (Mission Figs will work)

Remove stems from figs and cut in half; set aside.

4 teaspoons olive oil (preferably Spanish or Greek)

1 large yellow onion, chopped

2 cloves garlic, minced

1 cup full-bodied dry red wine

1 (14.5 ounce) can crushed tomatoes

½ cup venison stock (page 11) or beef broth

2 large carrots, cut into ¾-inch pieces

2 bay leaves

3 strips (¾ x 3-inch) lemon zest*

2 pounds venison stew meat, cut into cubes

¼ teaspoon salt

¼ teaspoon freshly ground black pepper

½ to ¾ cup quartered, pitted Kalamata olives

Chopped fresh thyme or Italian parsley

*Remove strips of lemon zest (yellow part only) with vegetable peeler.

Heat 2 teaspoons of the oil in large skillet over medium-high heat. Add one cube of venison and cook, turning to brown all sides. (Once cooked, remove the cube from the skillet and give your doggie a little treat.) Reduce the heat to medium and add remaining 2 teaspoons of oil to the skillet along with the onion and garlic. Stir and cook until the onion softens, about 5 minutes. Add wine, tomatoes, and broth to skillet. Simmer 1 minute, stirring with a wooden spoon.

Transfer mixture to slow cooker. Add figs, carrots, bay leaves and lemon zest. Cover and cook on low for 2 to 3 hours, or until vegetables are tender.

Sprinkle venison with salt and pepper and add to slow cooker. Cook for 20 to 30 minutes, or until the meat is tender.

Remove bay leaves and lemon zest. Stir in olives and sprinkle with thyme or parsley. Serve with rice.

{
Note:
Even devout meat and potatoes men like this—Rick deemed it "the best thing you've ever made."
}

Venison Shorba Soup

SERVES 4

Ingredients	*Directions*
1 tablespoon oil	Heat the oil in a stock pot and sauté the onions until soft, about 5 minutes. Add the crushed garlic and red pepper flakes and mix well. Add tomatoes, chick peas, water, and spices and sauté for 2 more minutes. Add the venison and simmer until the meat is cooked, but still tender (about 5 minutes). Reduce heat to low and stir in yogurt.
1 medium onion, chopped	
1 large clove garlic, crushed	
½ teaspoon dried red pepper flakes	
2 fresh tomatoes, skinned, seeded, and coarsely chopped	
1 can (19-ounce) chick peas, drained	
2 cups water	Serve immediately.
1 teaspoon cumin	
1 tablespoon chopped fresh mint	
½ teaspoon cinnamon	
½ teaspoon cardamom	
½ teaspoon salt	
3 sprigs saffron	
¾ pound venison kabob meat cut into small (½-inch) cubes	
½ cup Greek yogurt	

Tunisian Venison Tagine

SERVES 6

Ingredients	Directions
3 tablespoons virgin olive oil	Heat oil in a skillet over a medium-high heat. Sauté the parsnips, sweet potatoes, celery, and onion until lightly browned, about 4 minutes. Stir in garlic, cumin, coriander, and allspice. Cook until vegetables are coated, about 1 minute. Transfer vegetables to slow cooker.
5 parsnips, peeled and cut into chunks	
2 large sweet potatoes, peeled and cut into chunks	
½ cup celery, cut into 1-inch slices	
2 medium onions, cut into 1-inch cubes	
4 cloves garlic, minced	Put broth in skillet and bring to boil. Pour into slow cooker, including scrapings from pan. Add tomatoes, black pepper, cinnamon stick, and chili pepper to cooker. Cover and cook 6 to 8 hours on low, until fork tender.
1 tablespoon ground cumin	
1 tablespoon ground coriander	
½ teaspoon ground allspice	
1½ cups venison broth (page 11) or beef broth	
1 (15-ounce) can diced tomatoes, with juice	Season the venison with salt and put in slow cooker for an additional 10 minutes.
1 teaspoon black pepper, coarsely ground	
1 (3-inch) cinnamon stick	
1 dried red chili pepper	Mix almonds with lemon juice and zest in small bowl.
1 pound venison stew meat, cut into cubes	
½ teaspoon salt	Remove cinnamon stick and chili pepper from slow cooker. Stir in almond mixture and cook on high until slightly thickened, about 15 minutes.
¼ cup almonds, toasted and ground	
Juice and zest of ½ lemon	
¼ cup chopped Italian parsley	
	Serve stew on a bed of couscous or rice and sprinkle with parsley.

Venison and Wild Rice Soup

SERVES 6

Ingredients	Directions

Ingredients

4 cups venison stock (recipe page 11)

2 cups water

½ cup wild rice, uncooked

1 small red onion, chopped

4 ounces fresh mushrooms, sliced

1 cup frozen spinach

2 cloves garlic, minced

½ teaspoon ground sage

1 teaspoon salt

¼ teaspoon pepper

1 pound venison stew meat, cut into small cubes

Directions

Place broth, water, rice, and onion in a stockpot and bring to a boil. Reduce heat, cover, and simmer until rice is cooked (about 30 minutes). Add mushrooms, spinach, garlic, sage, salt, and pepper and simmer for 5 minutes. Add venison and cook on low until venison is tender, about 10 minutes. Serve immediately.

Fat Tuesday Jambalaya

SERVES 6

Ingredients	*Directions*
1 tablespoon oil	Heat oil in a large stew pot over medium-high heat. Add onion, bell pepper, garlic, and sausage. Sauté 5 minutes or until vegetables are tender.
1 cup chopped onion	
1 cup chopped red bell pepper	
1 tablespoon minced garlic	
½ pound andouille sausage, sliced (recipe page 66)	Add rice and the next 7 ingredients (through bay leaf) and sauté 2 minutes.
1 cup long-grain white rice, uncooked	
1 teaspoon paprika	Add broth, water, tomato paste, hot pepper sauce, and diced tomatoes; bring to a boil. Cover, reduce heat, and simmer 20 minutes.
1 teaspoon freshly ground black pepper	
1 teaspoon dried oregano	
½ teaspoon onion powder	Add shrimp; cook 5 minutes. Let stand 5 minutes. Discard bay leaf, stir in parsley, and serve.
½ teaspoon dried thyme	
¼ teaspoon garlic salt	
1 bay leaf	
2 cups venison stock (page 11) or chicken broth	
¾ cup water	
1 tablespoon tomato paste	
½ teaspoon hot pepper sauce	
1 (15-ounce) can, no salt-added diced tomatoes, with juice	
½ pound medium shrimp with tails, peeled and deveined	
2 tablespoons chopped fresh parsley	

I grew up thinking casserole was synonymous with cream of mushroom soup. My mother was the queen of pouring the soup over rice or noodles, adding some type of meat, topping it with potato chips, and baking it. I loved casserole night!

Imagine my surprise the first time I tasted cassoulet in a fine French restaurant. It was not like Mom's casserole—there was not a drop of cream of mushroom soup to be found in it.

According to the dictionary, a casserole is any collection of foods, usually meat and vegetables, heated in a broth or stock. Casseroles can be complicated, like the traditional cassoulet, or easy peasy, like Mom's tuna noodle casserole. But they have one thing in common—all ingredients are added to a casserole dish and cooked so that the flavors blend together. And they're delicious. Okay, that's two things in common.

Venison Lasagna

SERVES 8

Ingredients	Directions
15 ounces ricotta cheese	Preheat oven to 350°.
3 cups shredded mozzarella cheese	
½ cup grated Parmesan cheese	Combine cheeses and eggs in a bowl.
2 eggs, beaten	
4 cups Venison Meat Sauce (recipe page 65)	Spread about 1 cup sauce on bottom of baking pan. Layer 3 pieces of uncooked lasagna over sauce and cover with sauce. Spread cheese filling over sauce.
1½ cups water	
¼ teaspoon salt	
¼ teaspoon pepper	Repeat layers of lasagna, sauce, and cheese filling. Top with a layer of lasagna and remaining sauce.
8 ounces lasagna noodles, uncooked	
	Cover with aluminum foil and bake for 50 to 60 minutes. Remove foil; bake about 10 minutes longer. Allow to sit 10 minutes before cutting.

{ *Note:*
What is the difference between a stew and a casserole? With stews, heat is applied to the bottom of the cooking vessel, whereas casseroles are cooked in an oven where heat circulates all around the cooking vessel. }

Mock Lasagna

SERVES 8

Ingredients	Directions

Ingredients

3 to 4 cups Venison Meat Sauce (recipe page 65)

15 ounces ricotta cheese

2 cups shredded mozzarella cheese

1 cup shredded parmesan cheese

1 cup sliced mushrooms (optional)

1 pound rotini or ziti, cooked and drained

Directions

Preheat oven to 350°.

Mix the meat sauce, ricotta, mozzarella, and half of the parmesan in a large bowl. Add the mushrooms and mix, then add the pasta and mix until it is thoroughly coated with the sauce and cheese mixture. Spread the mixture in a baking dish. Sprinkle remaining parmesan cheese over top and place in oven, uncovered, for 30 to 40 minutes (until casserole is heated through). Let sit for 5 minutes and serve.

NOTE:
If you don't have any meat sauce in the freezer and you don't have time to make it, substitute it with ½ pound ground venison, browned, mixed with 1 (16-ounce) jar of your favorite pre-made tomato sauce.

Venison Stroganoff
SERVES 8

Ingredients	*Directions*
1 pound ground venison	Preheat oven to 350°. Spray a 13 by 9-inch baking dish with nonstick cooking spray.
¼ teaspoon salt	
⅛ teaspoon freshly ground black pepper	
1 teaspoon vegetable oil	Brown the venison, adding the salt and pepper. Remove meat from the skillet, then add oil to the skillet and heat over medium-high heat until hot. Add onion and garlic and cook until the onion is tender, about 5 minutes.
½ large onion, finely chopped	
3 cloves garlic, minced	
8 ounces sliced mushrooms	
¼ cup white wine	
1 can cream of mushroom or cream of chicken soup, undiluted	Add mushrooms and cook until tender. Add wine. Reduce heat to medium-low and simmer 3 minutes. Remove from heat and stir in soup, sour cream, and mustard until well combined. Return browned venison to skillet.
½ cup sour cream	
1 tablespoon Dijon mustard	
2 pounds egg noodles, cooked	
Chopped fresh parsley, optional	Add cooked noodles to skillet and stir until noodles are well coated. Pour into baking dish. Bake uncovered, 30 minutes or until heated through. Garnish with chopped parsley, if desired.

Venison and Artichoke Alfredo

SERVES 4

Ingredients	Directions
1 1-pound package egg noodles	Cook egg noodles. Drain and mix with 1 tablespoon of butter. Set aside.
2 tablespoons butter	
4 petite venison steaks (3 to 4 ounces each)	Preheat oven to 350°.
1 (15-ounce) jar Alfredo sauce with mushrooms	
½ cup artichoke hearts, quartered	Heat a skillet and melt the other tablespoon of butter. Brown the petite steaks, about 3 minutes on each side.
1 tablespoon capers	

Spread the egg noodles in a baking dish. Place meat on top of the noodles.

Combine Alfredo sauce, artichoke hearts, and capers in the skillet you used for browning the meat and heat. When heated through (about 1 minute), pour over meat and noodles.

Place, uncovered, in oven for 30 minutes, until the steaks are cooked through.

Enchiladas

SERVES 8

Ingredients	Directions
1 pound ground venison, browned (recipe page 9)	Preheat oven to 350°.
1 package taco seasoning mix	Mix browned meat, taco seasoning, beans, soup, onion, peppers, and rice together. Spoon about ¼ cup of the mixture on each tortilla. Roll the tortillas and place seam-side down into a shallow baking dish. Pour the enchilada sauce over the filled tortillas and sprinkle with cheese.
1 (16-ounce) can refried beans	
1 (10-ounce) can Cheddar Cheese Soup	
1 medium onion, chopped	
½ jar pickled chili peppers (mild or spicy, depending on preference)	
1 cup long-grain white rice, cooked	Bake for 20 minutes or until the enchiladas are hot and bubbling. Let sit for 5 minutes before serving.
12 (10-inch) flour tortillas, warmed	
1½ cup enchilada sauce, canned	
Shredded Cheddar cheese	Top with a dollop of sour cream.

Corn and Venison Casserole

SERVES 6

Ingredients	Directions

Ingredients

1 to 1½ pound neck roast

Venison stock (page 11) or chicken broth

1 carton (14-ounce) Southwestern style corn soup

1 small onion, diced

1 medium green bell pepper, diced

½ teaspoon chili powder

Tortilla chips, crumbled

1 cup shredded cheese (optional)

Directions

In the morning or the day before, put the roast in a slow cooker and cover completely with stock (you can add water to the stock to cover the roast). Cook on low setting 8 to 12 hours, until roast shreds easily with a fork. Remove the roast from the liquid and shred. Set aside (or refrigerate if you're making the casserole the next day).

Preheat oven to 350°.
In a mixing bowl combine soup, onion, pepper, and chili powder. Set aside.

Line an 8 by 8-inch baking dish with crumbled tortilla chips. Cover chips with meat and pour soup mixture over the meat. Bake for about 40 minutes, or until meat is heated through. Remove from oven. If serving with cheese, sprinkle the cheese on top and let melt before serving.

Spicy Southwestern Casserole
SERVES 8

Ingredients	*Directions*
1 pound ground venison, browned (recipe page 9) 1 (16-ounce) container Southwestern corn chowder 1 (15-ounce) container Ricotta cheese 2 cups rice, cooked 1 (12-ounce) can black beans (optional) 1 red pepper, diced 1 tablespoon hot sauce 1½ teaspoon salt ½ teaspoon cayenne pepper ¼ teaspoon pepper 1 cup Cheddar cheese, shredded Tortilla chips	Preheat oven to 325°. In a bowl, combine the browned venison, chowder, ricotta, rice, beans (if using), red pepper, hot sauce, salt, cayenne, and pepper and mix well. Spoon mixture into a baking dish. Sprinkle with Cheddar cheese. Place in oven and cook for 30 minutes, or until heated through. Let sit for 5 minutes before serving. Serve with tortilla chips.

Traditional Shepherd's Pie
SERVES 6

Ingredients	*Directions*
2 or 3 carrots, peeled and chopped into ¼-inch pieces 1 tablespoon oil 1 pound ground venison 1 onion, chopped 1 shallot, chopped 1 clove garlic, chopped ½ cup frozen green peas ½ cup sliced mushrooms 8 ounces tomato sauce 1½ to 2 teaspoons salt 2 teaspoons Worcestershire sauce ½ teaspoon sage ½ teaspoon thyme 3 cups creamy mashed potatoes	Preheat oven to 350°. Place the carrots in a steamer and steam until tender, about 15 minutes. Meanwhile, heat the oil over high heat in a large skillet. Reduce temperature to medium and add the ground venison, onion, shallot, and garlic; cook and stir until meat is cooked. Drain off any grease. Stir in the carrots, peas, mushrooms, and tomato sauce. Add salt, Worcestershire sauce, sage, and thyme. Transfer mixture to a greased 8-inch baking dish. Spread mashed potatoes over the top of the casserole and bake uncovered for 25 minutes, until the top is browned and the casserole is heated through.

Upside Down Shepherd's Pie
SERVES 6

Ingredients	*Directions*
1 tablespoon oil 1 medium onion, chopped finely 1 clove garlic, minced 1 teaspoon oregano 1/2 teaspoon basil 1 pound ground venison 2 eggs ½ cup bread crumbs ½ cup tomato sauce 1 tablespoon balsamic vinegar ½ teaspoon salt ¼ teaspoon pepper 3 cups creamy mashed potatoes	Preheat oven to 350°. Heat the oil in a skillet. Sauté the onion and garlic in the oil until tender, about 5 minutes. Combine onions and all other ingredients (except potatoes) in a large mixing bowl. Use your hands to make sure everything is mixed thoroughly. Put the meat mixture in a baking pan. Press along sides to create a shell. Fill shell with potatoes. Place in oven, uncovered, and cook for 50 to 60 minutes, until meat is cooked through. Let sit 5 to 10 minutes before serving.

Vaquero Pie

SERVES 4 TO 6

Ingredients	Directions

2 tablespoons oil

1 large sweet onion, finely chopped

2 cloves garlic, minced

3 cups tomatoes, diced

2 cups venison stock (page 11) or chicken broth

1 cup frozen corn kernels

½ teaspoon cayenne pepper

1 pound venison stew meat, cubed

1 cup shitake mushrooms, sliced

½ teaspoon ground cumin

1 teaspoon sea salt

Pepper to taste

1 package cornbread mix

In a sauté pan, heat the oil over medium high heat. Add onion and cook until tender, about 5 minutes. Add the garlic and cook 1 minute. Add half of the tomatoes, turn the heat to low, and simmer for 20 minutes.

Preheat oven to 350°.

Put the stock in a sauce pan and bring to a boil. Add the corn and a dash of the cayenne pepper and cook for 1 minute. Add the venison and mushrooms and cook for another 3 minutes. Add remaining tomatoes, cayenne pepper, cumin, salt, and pepper and mix well. Stir in the onion mixture.

Prepare the cornbread mixture according to package directions. Set aside.

Scoop the venison mixture into an 8 by 8-inch baking dish. (Save the excess liquid for something else, like a nice bowl of noodle soup.) Dollop the corn bread mix on top of the casserole.

Bake until cornbread is brown on top, about 20 minutes. Let sit for 5 minutes before serving.

Scottish Mince Pie
SERVES 6

Ingredients	*Directions*

Ingredients

1½ pounds ground venison

4 cups water to cover

1 large onion, chopped finely

1/8 teaspoon beef bouillon granules

Salt and pepper

¼ cup water

2 tablespoons cornstarch

½ cup frozen peas

2 (9-inch) pastry crusts

Directions

Preheat oven to 375°.
Place the ground venison in a large pot and pour in enough water to cover it. Boil until venison is cooked through. Drain off about a cup of the water—you want just enough left to cover the meat. Add onion and enough bouillon granules to add some taste. Cook until the onions are soft, about 5 minutes. Season with salt and pepper to taste.

Combine ¼ cup water with cornstarch and stir until smooth. Add to the venison mixture and cook until mixture has thickened. Add peas to mixture and mix well.

Pour venison mixture into one pastry crust and cover the top with the other crust. Crimp edges and prick top. Bake for 30 minutes, or until crust is lightly browned. Remove from oven and let sit for 10 minutes before serving.

CASSEROLES AND

Three Cheese Pasta and Venison

SERVES 8

Ingredients	Directions
1 (16-ounce) package rotini	Prepare rotini according to directions, drain, and set aside.
1 pound ground venison, browned (recipe page 9)	
1 (10-ounce) jar Alfredo sauce	Preheat oven to 350°.
1 (8-ounce) container sour cream	Stir together the browned meat, Alfredo sauce, and sour cream. Toss with rotini until evenly coated. Spoon half of mixture into a lightly greased baking dish. Stir together ricotta cheese, eggs, Parmesan, and parsley. Spread mixture over pasta in baking dish. Cover with remaining pasta. Sprinkle evenly with Mozzarella cheese. Bake for 30 minutes or until bubbly. Let sit for 5 minutes before serving.
1 (15-ounces) container ricotta cheese	
2 large eggs	
¼ cup Parmesan cheese, grated	
¼ cup chopped fresh parsley	
1½ cups grated mozzarella cheese	

Venison and Smoked Gouda Strata

SERVES 6

Ingredients	*Directions*

Ingredients

1 tablespoon olive oil
1 pound venison (backstrap), cut into thin slices
1 cup milk
½ cup dry white wine
1 loaf day-old French bread, cut into ½-inch slices
2 cups chopped fresh cilantro
3 tablespoons olive oil
½ pound smoked Gouda cheese, thinly sliced
3 ripe tomatoes, thinly sliced
1/2 cup basil pesto
4 eggs
Salt and pepper
½ cup whipping cream

Directions

Prep this dish the day before you plan to serve it. It needs to refrigerate overnight.

Heat the olive oil in a skillet over medium-high heat. Pan-sear the venison. Set aside.

Lightly grease an 8 by 8-inch baking dish. In a shallow bowl, combine milk and wine. Dip bread, 1 or 2 slices at a time, in milk mixture. Gently squeeze as much liquid as possible from bread, taking care not to tear. Place bread in baking dish. Cover bread with the meat, sprinkle cilantro over the meat, and drizzle with olive oil. Layer half of the cheese and half of the tomato slices on top. Top with half of the pesto. Repeat layers of cheese, tomato, and pesto. In medium bowl, beat eggs and season with salt and pepper. Pour evenly over layered mixture. Carefully pour cream over top and cover with plastic wrap. Chill overnight. About 3 hours before serving, remove strata from the refrigerator and bring to room temperature.

Preheat oven to 350°.
Bake, uncovered, until puffy and browned (about 1 hour). Let sit for 5 to 10 minutes before serving.

Did you know that the average American eats three burgers a week? And if they're not eating a burger, they're likely eating meat loaf, tacos, or something else that calls for grinding the meat. I'll eat burgers any way they come, but venison burgers are my favorite. In fact, ground venison in anything is amazing. It's got the rich flavor of red meat with the low-fat content of turkey—a fantastic combination.

Good Old American Burger

SERVES 3 TO 4

Ingredients	*Directions*
1 pound ground venison 1 to 2 tablespoons oil (canola, peanut, or whatever you like) 1 teaspoon Worcestershire sauce Salt and pepper to taste Nonstick spray	Preheat grill to 350° or preheat broiler. Mix all ingredients together, except the nonstick spray. Form meat into four patties. If grilling, spray the grill with nonstick spray. Cook patties about 4 minutes per side (depending on how you like them).

BBQ Venison Burger

SERVES 6

Ingredients	*Directions*
1¼ pounds ground venison (chilled) ¼ cup sweet onion, chopped fine 1 clove garlic, minced 2 tablespoons finely chopped fresh Italian parsley ¼ cup dry red wine ¼ cup BBQ sauce ¼ cup fine bread crumbs	Preheat grill. Mix all ingredients together in a bowl. Form meat into patties. You should be able to make 4 to 6, depending on how big you like your burgers. Put on grill and cook each side 4 to 6 minutes, or until done. Melt Cheddar cheese on top if desired.

Classic Blue Burger

SERVES 4

Ingredients	Directions
1 pound ground venison Olive oil 3 ounces crumbled blue cheese* *You can substitute the blue cheese with gorgonzola as well.*	Preheat grill. Mix venison and olive oil, and form into 8 thin burger patties. Place ¼ of the cheese on a patty. Place another patty on top and pinch the sides together. Repeat. Grill for about 3 minutes per side or until the meat is cooked to your preference. Putting the cheese inside the meat does two things: it keeps the bleu cheese crumbles from falling off the burger and the cheese helps hold the venison meat together on the grill.

Spicy Burgers

SERVES 3 TO 4

Ingredients	Directions
1 pound ground venison ½ teaspoon salt 1 onion, finely chopped 1 egg, beaten 2 teaspoons ground cumin ½ teaspoon ground allspice ½ teaspoon cayenne pepper ⅓ cup chopped cilantro	Preheat grill to 350° or preheat broiler. Put all ingredients in a food processor and process until well blended. Make the meat mixture in the morning and let it sit all day for spices to mingle (you don't have to, but if you can, do. Or make them as far in advance as you can). Shape into 3 or 4 patties. Cook on hot grill for about 4 minutes per side, or until the burgers are cooked to your liking. Serve with sour cream.

Hush Burgers

SERVES 4 TO 6

Ingredients	Directions
1¼ pound ground venison	Preheat grill to 325°.
½ cup oat or corn meal, finely ground	Mash the corn well using either a mortar and pestle or a food processor. Mix all ingredients thoroughly. Form into 4 to 6 burgers, depending on how large you want them.
½ cup grated Cheddar cheese	
½ cup corn kernels, frozen or canned	
¼ cup diced onion	
1 teaspoon Worcestershire sauce	Spray grill with nonstick spray. Put on grill and cook each side about 4 minutes, or until cooked to your preference. Serve with fresh salsa.
½ teaspoon salt	

Oat Burgers

SERVES 4 TO 5

Ingredients	Directions
1 pound ground venison	Preheat grill to 325°.
2 tablespoons steak sauce	Mix all ingredients together in large bowl. Form into 4 or 5 patties.
1 tablespoon honey	
¼ cup quick oats, uncooked	Spray grill with nonstick cooking spray. Cook for 4 minutes per side, or until the burgers are cooked to your liking. Baste with steak sauce while cooking.

Horseradish Burgers

SERVES 4 TO 5

Ingredients	Directions
1 to 1¼ pounds ground venison	Preheat grill to 325°.
¼ cup chopped onion	Mix all ingredients together in large bowl. Form into 4 or 5 patties.
1 tablespoon prepared horseradish	
1 teaspoon kosher salt	Spray grill with nonstick cooking spray. Cook for 4 minutes per side, or until the burgers are cooked to your liking. Serve on toasted bun with a slice of Cheddar and tomato.
2 teaspoons brown mustard	
1 dash pepper	

Irish Style Meat Loaf
SERVES 8 TO 10

Ingredients	Directions
2 eggs 3 cups fine bread crumbs 1 red pepper 1 large onion 1½ pounds ground venison ½ pound ground pork	Preheat oven to 350°. Put eggs, bread crumbs, red pepper, and onion in a food processor and pulse until well mixed. Put in a bowl with the meat and mix thoroughly (use a stand mixer with the hook attachment or mix with your hands). Spread mixture in a loaf pan. Bake for 1 hour. Remove from oven and pour off the fat, if any. Cover and cook for another hour. Remove from oven and let sit for 5 minutes before serving.

Good Old American Meat Loaf
SERVES 6 TO 8

Ingredients	Directions
1 pound ground venison ½ pound ground beef 1 cup milk (whole or 2%) 1 large egg, beaten ¼ teaspoon dried parsley ¼ teaspoon dried thyme ½ teaspoon dried basil ¼ teaspoon freshly ground pepper 2 cloves garlic, minced 1 small onion, finely chopped ½ cup dry bread crumbs ½ cup ketchup	Preheat oven to 350°. Combine all ingredients in a large bowl, and mix well, using a stand mixer or your hands to really get the ingredients mixed together. Place mixture into an ungreased loaf pan and bake uncovered until no pink remains at the center of the meat loaf, about 1½ hours. Remove from oven and let sit for 5 minutes. Remove from pan and slice to serve. Serve with ketchup or BBQ sauce drizzled on each slice.

Appalachian Meat Loaf

SERVES 6 TO 8

Ingredients	*Directions*
1 pound ground venison 1 pound ground pork 1 cup bread crumbs 1 medium onion, finely chopped ¼ cup evaporated milk 1 large egg, beaten ½ cup spicy BBQ sauce ½ teaspoon salt ¼ teaspoon pepper ½ cup ketchup 1 tablespoon BBQ sauce	Preheat oven to 350°. Combine venison, pork, bread crumbs, and onion and mix well. Mix with a stand mixer or your hands to make sure ingredients are well blended. Add the milk, egg, BBQ sauce, salt, pepper, and half of the ketchup to meat mixture and combine well. Put in a loaf pan and bake for 30 minutes. Mix remaining ketchup and BBQ sauce. Spread over loaf and bake 1 hour or until done. Let sit for 5 minutes before serving.

Mexicali Meat Loaf

SERVES 6 TO 8

Ingredients	*Directions*
1 (10-ounce) can red enchilada sauce 2 pounds ground venison 1 egg 1½ cup crushed corn chips ¼ to ½ cup shredded Cheddar cheese Cooked rice Avocado wedges Tomato wedges	Preheat oven to 350°. Put enchilada sauce, ground venison, egg, and corn chips in a bowl and mix thoroughly. Put meat mixture into a springform pan and bake for 50 minutes. Remove from oven and sprinkle cheese around edge of pan. Let stand 10 minutes. Remove side of pan and cut meat into wedge-shaped pieces. Arrange wedges on bed of hot cooked rice and garnish with tomato and avocado.

Twice-Baked Potatoes
SERVES 6

Ingredients	Directions
6 large Russet potatoes	Preheat the oven to 350°.
2 tablespoons butter	Scrub the potatoes and dry with paper towel.
1 pound ground venison, browned (page 9)	Using a fork, work your way around each potato
½ large onion, chopped finely	and poke holes. Place on baking sheet and bake
2 eggs, lightly beaten	for about 1 hour, or until soft inside. Remove
4 tablespoons BBQ sauce	from the oven and let cool for about an hour.
1 teaspoon salt	
Ground black pepper to taste	Slice the potatoes in half lengthwise. Scoop out
12 thin slices cheddar cheese	the insides, leaving the skins as shells. Place
2 teaspoons dried parsley	shells in a baking dish and set aside.

Preheat oven to 400°.
In a large mixing bowl, mash the potatoes with the butter. Stir in the venison, eggs, BBQ sauce, salt, and pepper and mix thoroughly. Spoon the mixture into the potato shells and bake for 30 minutes. Remove from the oven. Place a slice of cheese on each potatoes and sprinkle with parsley. Place back in over until cheese melts.

NOTE: *You may want to add more butter and/or cream to the mashed potatoes...it depends on your preference.*

Yummy-in-the-Tummy Venison Pot Pie

SERVES 4

Ingredients	Directions
1 pound venison stew meat, cubed	Brown venison with onion and set aside.
1 small onion, chopped	
½ cup frozen peas	Preheat oven to 425°.
2 carrots, peeled and sliced	In a medium bowl, mix together vegetables, soup, milk, and venison. Mix well. Place the
1 small potato, peeled and cubed	pie crust into four individual pot pie tins and pour mixture into pie crusts. Place second crust
1 (10-ounce) can cream of potato soup	on top of each and pinch edges together. Cut
½ cup milk	four slits in center of crust. Bake for 25 to 30
2 (9-inch) prepared pie crusts (or make them from scratch if you're so inclined)	minutes, until crust is golden brown. Let sit for 5 minutes before serving.

Venison Calzone

SERVES 2

Ingredients	Directions
1 tablespoon oil	Preheat oven to 400°.
1 pound ground venison	Heat the oil in a sauce pan and add the venison, green pepper, fennel, salt and pepper to brown.
½ green pepper, chopped	When cooked through, set aside.
1 teaspoon fennel seed	
1 teaspoon salt	Roll out dough, making an oblong shape about
¼ teaspoon pepper	¼ inch thick. Spread tomato sauce down one side of the dough. Top with venison and green
Pizza dough (either homemade or store bought, enough for 1 pizza)	pepper mixture, mozzarella, and romano cheese. Fold the uncovered portion of dough over the
1 (15-ounce) can tomato sauce	filling, and press the edges together with a fork
4 ounces mozzarella cheese, shredded	to seal. Brush with egg and sprinkle with sesame.
1 cup romano cheese	Bake in a bread pan until golden brown, about
1 egg, beaten	15 minutes. Cool 5 minutes, slice, and serve.
1 tablespoon sesame seeds	

Venison Meat Sauce

Ingredients

3 tablespoons olive oil

1 large sweet onion, chopped

1 or 2 cloves garlic, minced (depending on how much garlic you like)

1½ to 2 pounds ground venison

1 teaspoon paprika

1 (28-ounce) can diced tomatoes (with liquid)

1 (15-ounce) can tomato sauce

1 (12-ounce) can tomato paste

½ cup red wine

1 tablespoon dried basil

¼ teaspoon cayenne pepper

¼ teaspoon oregano

3 tablespoons dried parsley

1 teaspoon kosher salt

Pepper to taste

Directions

Heat the olive oil and sauté the onion until translucent (about 5 minutes). Add the garlic and sauté another minute. Add the ground meat and paprika and cook until meat is browned. Add the remaining ingredients and simmer for 1 to 4 hours (the sauce is ready to eat after 1 hour, but will be better the longer it simmers).

NOTE: *I usually make double batches and freeze it. It is wonderful to have on hand for a quick lasagna in the winter, or even just good old spaghetti.*

Nurenburg Style Brats

MAKES 9 POUNDS

Ingredients	Directions
5 pounds venison 4 pounds pork fat 8 teaspoons salt 4 tablespoons white pepper 4 tablespoons caraway seed 2 teaspoons ground mace Small, natural sausage casings	Run venison through the meat grinder, then run it through the grinder again with the pork fat. Using your hands or the hook attachment on your stand mixer, mix the spices into the meat thoroughly. Stuff the sausage casings according to the directions on your sausage stuffer, making sure the brats are no more than 1¼ inch in diameter. Once a casing is stuffed, tie it off at about 4 inches long. Grill or broil and serve with spicy brown mustard, sauerkraut, and hard rolls. *These brats freeze well, so make a lot of them!*

Andouille Sausage

MAKES I POUND

Ingredients	Directions
½ pound ground venison ½ pound ground pork ½ tablespoon coarse salt ⅓ teaspoon cayenne ½ teaspoon rubbed sage ½ teaspoon ground cloves ½ teaspoon ground mace ½ teaspoon ground allspice ½ teaspoon freshly ground black pepper ½ teaspoon ground bayleaf 1 pinch thyme ½ clove garlic, crushed Large, natural sausage casings	Grind the venison and pork coarsely, using a 3/8" plate. Mix in the spices, using your hands to mix thoroughly. Use the sausage stuffing attachment to stuff into casings. You want the sausage to be about 1¼ inches thick. Place the sausage in a smoker with hickory chips, or use your gas grill (instructions, page 10). Smoke slowly until the sausages reach 175°, which should be about 2 hours. Eat immediately or freeze. Don't smoke them too fast, or they'll shrink and get wrinkled.

Flavorful Venison Breakfast Sausage
SERVES 4 TO 8

Ingredients	Directions
1 pound venison	Put the venison through the meat grinder with the pork fat so that it is well mixed. Mix in other ingredients, using your hands to blend well.
½ pound pork fat	
½ tablespoon kosher salt	
½ teaspoon rubbed sage	
⅓ teaspoon rubbed summer savory	Form into 1- or 2-ounce patties. Cook on skillet.
⅛ teaspoon ground nutmeg	
⅔ teaspoon ground marjoram	
⅓ teaspoon freshly ground black pepper	*These freeze well. I place wax paper between each patty so that I can easily separate them once they've thawed.*

I grew up eating roast on Sunday and roast beef sandwiches on Monday! I always loved roast night, but I never gave it much thought as to why my family—and every other family I knew—ate roast on Sunday. It turns out that Sunday roast is a British tradition dating back to when the squire would treat his serfs to a meal of roast oxen every Sunday to reward them for the week's work. I wonder if the squire shared the leftovers.

Salt Roast

SERVES 4 TO 10, DEPENDING ON SIZE OF ROAST

Ingredients	Directions
1 (2- to 5-pound) boneless venison roast **5-pound bag coarse salt** **Water** **Meat thermometer** *Picture on the left*	Preheat oven to 200°. Pour the salt in a bowl and add water until the salt is moist. You don't want it dripping wet; you just need the salt wet enough to hold together a little when you cover the roast. Put the roast in a roasting pan and cover with the salt. Make sure the entire roast is covered with the salt mixture (it is a little messy). Place on the center rack and cook for about 2 hours, until the internal temperature is about 15 degrees lower than how you like your meat (for example, pull it out of the oven at 120° and let the meat sit until the internal temperature reaches 135° for rare or 145° for medium, depending on how you like it). Remove from the oven and let sit. When you're ready to carve, you'll be able to chisel through the salt and move the roast to a cutting board. You can cook it at higher temperatures for shorter time periods; just follow the general roast cooking times. The salt casing will slow your cooking time, so make sure to use the meat thermometer. We use the lower temperature because the meat comes out more evenly cooked.

> **NOTE:**
> *I get my coarse salt at the local international market. I've never seen large bags of coarse eating salt at a regular grocery store. You have to use the coarse salt; table salt won't work.*

Simple Oven Roast

SERVES 4 TO 10, DEPENDING ON SIZE OF ROAST

Ingredients	Directions
1 teaspoon sea salt or kosher salt Pepper to taste ¼ cup olive oil 1 (2- to 5-pound) boneless venison shoulder roast	Preheat oven to 200°. Put the salt, pepper, and olive oil in a small bowl and mix well. Rub the roast with the mixture, using your hands to massage the oil into the meat. Place the roast in a roasting pan and cook uncovered until it reaches 125° inside (about 1 to 3 hours, depending on the size of the roast). Remove from oven and let the meat sit until the internal temperature reaches 135° (rare) or 145° (medium), depending on how you like your meat.

Garlic and Herb Roast

SERVES 4 TO 10, DEPENDING ON SIZE OF ROAST

Ingredients	Directions

6 to 12 cloves garlic (depending on size of roast)

1 (2- to 5-pound) boneless venison shoulder roast

1 to 2 tablespoons finely chopped fresh thyme

1 to 2 tablespoons finely chopped fresh sage

1 to 2 tablespoons finely chopped fresh rosemary

1 teaspoon sea salt or kosher salt

Pepper to taste

¼ cup olive oil

Preheat oven to 200°.
Peel the garlic cloves and slice in quarters.
Make 1-inch slits in the roast and insert the garlic in the slits—put them all over roast, top and bottom.

Combine the herbs (anywhere from 2 tablespoons to ¼ cup, depending on the size of the roast), salt, pepper, and olive oil in a small bowl and mix well. Rub the roast with the herb mixture, using your hands to massage the oil into the meat.

Place the roast in a roasting pan and cook uncovered until its internal temperature reaches 125° (about 1 to 3 hours, depending on the size of the roast).

Remove from oven and let the meat sit until the internal temperature reaches 135° (rare) or 145° (medium), depending on how you like your meat.

Apple Rotisserie Roast

SERVES 6 TO 8

Ingredients	Directions
2 cups apple cider	Combine all ingredients, except the roast and water, in a large bowl. Place the roast in a large pot—big enough to fit the roast and have room for the liquid. Pour the marinade over it. Add enough water so that the marinade covers the roast completely. Place in refrigerator and marinate overnight (or about 10 to 12 hours).
½ cup apple cider vinegar	
¼ cup Worcestershire sauce	
½ teaspoon ginger	
1 apple, diced	
½ onion, chopped	
1 (2- to 4-pound) boneless venison shoulder roast	Preheat grill to 225°.
Water	Put roast on rotisserie. Grill for 2 to 3 hours, until roast reaches an internal temperature of 125°. Remove from rotisserie and let the meat sit until the internal temperature reaches 135° (rare) or 145° (medium).

Chipotle Venison Roast

SERVES 6 TO 8

Ingredients	*Directions*
1 or 2 venison neck roasts (about 2 pounds)	Put the roast in a slow cooker. Add all ingredients, along with just enough water to cover the roast. Cook on low setting for 8 to 12 hours, until the meat falls apart when pierced with a fork.
2 cups venison stock (or whatever stock you have)	
1 (15-ounce) can diced tomatoes (with liquid)	
2 chipotle peppers in adobo sauce (about 2 tablespoons)	
1 yellow bell pepper, quartered	Serve this as a roast with veggies on the side, or as a stew (the broth is delicious).
1 medium onion, quartered	
Water	

Venison Slow Cooker Pot Roast

SERVES 6 TO 8

Ingredients	*Directions*
1 (2- to 4-pound) venison roast	Trim any silver off the roast (instructions page 6). Rub some steak rub onto the meat. Place the roast in the slow cooker. Add vegetables. Cover the roast and vegetables with the stock. Cook on low setting for 8 to 12 hours, until the meat falls apart when pierced with a fork. (Cooking time will depend on the size of the roast.)
Steak rub seasoning blend	
2 carrots, cut in ½-inch pieces	
1 onion, quartered	
2 potatoes, cut in 1- to 2-inch cubes	
Venison, chicken, or beef stock (enough to cover roast and vegetables in the cooker)	

> **NOTE:**
> *Slow cookers are great for the not-so-nice cuts of meat. Cooking them all day long takes them past the point of tough and back to tender again.*

Reindeer with Lingonberry Sauce

SERVES 6 TO 8

Ingredients	Directions
1 orange, juiced plus finely chopped peel	Heat the wine in a small sauce pan and add the orange peel. Cook over medium high heat until the wine is reduced by one-third. Lower the heat to medium and add the orange juice, lemon juice, lingonberry preserves, and ginger paste. Stir until preserves have melted.
1 cup Port wine	
1 tablespoon freshly squeezed lemon juice	
½ cup lingonberry preserves (you can use cranberry preserves if you can't find lingonberry)	
⅛ teaspoon ginger paste	Slice roast and serve with 1 tablespoon of the lingonberry sauce.
1 (2- to 5-pound) boneless venison shoulder roast, prepared using Salt Roast recipe (page 69)	
	This sauce can be served hot or cold. It will yield about 1 cup, which is plenty for 6 to 8 guests.

Corned Venison

SERVES 4 TO 12

Ingredients	Directions
2 quarts of spring or distilled water	*Make the brine*: Mix all ingredients except the venison roast in a stock pot. Heat to high and dissolve the ingredients, bring to a boil for 2 minutes. Turn off the stove and let the brine cool (this will take a few hours).
½ cup of canning or pickling salt	
½ cup of tenderizing salt	
3 tablespoons sugar	
1 tablespoon black peppercorns, cracked	
1 tablespoon coriander seeds	Put the roast in a container large enough to hold it and cover it with the brine. You can use a plastic storage container or a stock pot—whatever you have that is large enough and fits in your refrigerator. Submerge the meat completely; you may want to put a clean stone or other weight on it to ensure it stays submerged. Marinate the meat for 3 – 10 days in the refrigerator, depending on the size of the roast (larger cuts of meat take longer to corn. A 1-pound roast may take 3 days, a 5-pound roast 10 days. Err on the side of too long. You can also inject the brine mixture into the center area of the meat with a meat pump or syringe).
6 bay leaves, crushed	
1 tablespoon red pepper flakes	
1 tablespoon dried thyme	
1 teaspoon caraway seeds	
3 cloves garlic, chopped	
1 3 – 5 pound venison roast (shoulder or rump)	

When done marinating, drain off the brine solution and wash the meat with fresh water.

Place the meat in a pot and cover it with water. Be sure the pot you cook in isn't too large; you want the roast covered with water, but not swimming in the pot, otherwise you'll lose some of the flavor during cooking. Simmer on low for 3 – 5 hours, depending on the size of the roast.

Gigot de Venaison

SERVES 8 TO 10

Ingredients	Directions
4-pound shank end leg or 4-pound shoulder, bone in and trimmed	Preheat oven to 200°. Rub meat with oil and season with salt and pepper. Heat a 6-quart Dutch oven over medium-high heat. Add meat and cook, turning occasionally until browned on all sides, about 10 minutes. Transfer to a plate.
3 tablespoons olive oil	
Sea salt and freshly ground black pepper	
1 bottle dry white wine	
2 cups water	Add wine and water to the Dutch oven; bring to a boil and scrape up browned bits from bottom of pot.
20 cloves garlic, peeled	
10 sprigs each: rosemary, thyme, savory	
5 bay leaves	Nestle garlic and herbs into a large oval casserole; place meat on top and pour wine mixture over it. Put in oven, uncovered. Roast, basting frequently, for 4 hours. Uncover, flip meat, and continue to cook, basting frequently, until venison is very tender—8 to 10 hours. Transfer to a rack and cool for 20 minutes. Put cooking juices in gravy boat and serve with meat.

NOTE: *This roast will be done at 2 or 3 hours, but the longer you cook it, the more tender it will become. Make sure you baste frequently since the venison is so lean. It needs the basting to stay tender.*

Traditional Yankee Pot Roast

SERVES 6 TO 10

Ingredients	Directions
2 teaspoons olive oil	Preheat oven to 200°.
4-pound boneless venison shoulder roast	Heat olive oil in a large Dutch oven over medium-high heat. Rub roast with salt and pepper. Add roast to pan, browning on all sides (about 3 minutes per side). Remove from pan. Add onion to pan and sauté until browned. Return roast to pan. Combine broth, ketchup, and Worcestershire and pour over roast. Add tomatoes; bring to a simmer. Add potatoes and carrots. Cover and bake for about 1 ½ hours, or until meat reaches 125° inside and vegetables are tender. Remove from oven. Stir in lemon juice and let sit 10 to 15 minutes (until the internal temperature reaches 135° for rare or 145° for medium). Garnish with parsley, if desired.
1 tablespoon salt	
1 tablespoon freshly ground black pepper	
2 cups onion, coarsely chopped	
2 cups venison stock (page 11) or beef broth	
¼ cup ketchup	
2 tablespoons Worcestershire sauce	
1 cup plum tomatoes, chopped	
1¼ pounds small potatoes (red or gold, your preference)	
1 pound carrots, peeled and cut into 1-inch pieces	
2 tablespoons freshly squeezed lemon juice	
Chopped fresh parsley (optional)	

Rotisserie Roast with Garlic Rub

SERVES 4 TO 8

Ingredients	Directions
1 head of garlic	Peel each clove of garlic and put in mortar with salt. Grind until garlic and salt make a paste. Mix in the olive oil. Rub the roast with the garlic mixture. Put on rotisserie and grill for about 1 hour, until meat is 125° inside. Let the meat sit until the internal temperature reaches 135° (rare) or 145° (medium), about 10 minutes.
2 teaspoons coarse salt	
1 tablespoon olive oil	
1 (2- to 4-pound) boneless roast	

Nutty Venison Saddle in Bacon

SERVES 8

Ingredients	Directions
½ cup pepitas (raw pumpkin seeds)	Preheat oven to 200°.
½ cup sunflower seeds	Put seeds and nuts in a food processor and chop until they're the consistency of bread crumbs. Add the salt and pepper to the nuts and mix thoroughly. Spread the nuts in a shallow pan, one large enough to fit the saddle. Rub the venison saddle with the egg yolks. Roll the meat in the nuts so that the nuts form a crust. Spread about 10 slices of bacon in a row on a cutting board. Place the saddle on the bacon, then wrap each slice around the meat and secure it with toothpicks.
½ cup macadamia nuts	
1 teaspoon salt	
¼ teaspoon pepper	
4 pounds Venison Saddle*	
2 egg yolks, beaten	
1 pound uncured bacon	
1 tablespoon olive oil	

* This recipe would work well with a nice roast if you don't have a saddle or don't want to have to carve around a bone. You'll just need to adjust the cooking time; a boneless roast should take less time to cook.

Heat the oil in a large skillet over medium high heat. Brown the meat on each side, about 4 minutes per side. When the meat is browned, transfer the saddle to a roasting dish and place in oven. Cook until the internal temperature of the meat is 125°, about 2 hours.

Remove from oven and let the meat sit until the internal temperature reaches 135° (rare) or 145° (medium). Carve the meat from the bone to serve.

WHAT'S A SADDLE?
Ever had chops? Well, the saddle is the part of the animal that becomes your chops. It's the backstrap and tenderloin with the bone in. This is the best meat on the animal, which makes this dish a fabulous gourmet dinner. It's a little tough to get a saddle if you're butchering at home, but if you're willing to bring out the bone saw, it's worth the effort.

Grilled Tenderloin Medallions

SERVES 2 TO 4

Ingredients	Directions
Venison tenderloin/backstrap (enough for 3 to 6 ounces of meat per person) **Olive oil** **Steak rub**	Slice meat into 2-inch thick medallions (they should be about 2 ounces each). Make sure the pieces are uniform in size so that they cook at the same rate. Coat a baking pan with olive oil and place the medallions in it, turning to coat both sides.

Heat the grill. Rub a little of the steak rub on each side of meat (amount depends on how peppery you want the meat...we don't use much). Grill the meat to medium rare (the meat should just be getting firm when you bounce the spatula on it, about 2 or 3 minutes per side). Be sure to take the meat off the grill quickly: the tenderloin is best rare or medium rare. Serve quickly...the medallions cool fast. We usually warm the dinner plates to keep the meat hot. |

Loin Chops with Cranberry Orange Relish

SERVES 4

Ingredients	*Directions*
1 (12-ounce) package fresh cranberries 1 orange 1/2 teaspoon ginger paste (optional) 3/4 to 1 cup white sugar (depending on how sweet you like it) 2 tablespoons olive oil 1 teaspoon pepper rub 4 venison loin chops	Wash the cranberries and scrub the orange. Quarter the orange and remove seeds (leave the peel on). Put cranberries and orange in a food processor and pulse until coarsely chopped. Stop and scrape down sides of bowl, if necessary, to chop evenly. Add the ginger paste and sugar, taste to adjust the sweetness as desired. Stir well and refrigerate for at least 2 hours before serving. Preheat oven to broil. Mix the olive oil and pepper rub together in a small dish. Place the chops on a broiling pan and baste with the olive oil mixture. Broil for 3 to 4 minutes. Remove from oven, flip over, baste, and put under broiler for another 3 to 4 minutes. Remove from oven and serve immediately with relish.

Limey Beer Steak

SERVES 4

Ingredients	*Directions*
1 pound flank steak 2 cups low-sodium V8 vegetable juice 1 (12-ounce) light beer Juice of 1 lime	Put steak in container and pour other ingredients over it, cover, and marinate in refrigerator for 1 to 2 hours. Preheat grill to 325°. Remove meat from marinade and slice in ½-inch strips and place back in marinade for a few minutes. Place meat on the grill and cook for about 3 minutes, then flip and cook for another 3 minutes, or until meat is slightly firm to the touch. Serve immediately.

Sage Steak

SERVES 4

Ingredients	*Directions*
1 pound flank steak 1/2 cup chopped fresh sage 1 clove garlic, minced 1 tablespoon chopped fresh tarragon 1/4 cup olive oil 1-1/2 tablespoons Worcestershire sauce 1-1/2 tablespoons white wine vinegar Salt and pepper to taste	Butterfly the meat (instructions page 10) with a mallet on both sides until the meat flattens out to about ¼ inch. Place in a covered dish. Mix together the remaining ingredients, pour over meat, and marinade in refrigerator for 2 hours. Heat a skillet and pan-fry the steaks in the juices from the marinade, about 4 minutes on each side. Slice the steak into strips and arrange on platter. Serve with creamy mashed potatoes.

Savory Kabobs
SERVES 4

Ingredients	Directions
½ cup dry red wine 2 teaspoons dried onion 2 tablespoons vegetable oil 1 clove garlic, minced ¼ teaspoon pepper ¼ cup steak sauce 1½ pounds venison kabob meat, cut into 2-inch cubes	Combine wine, onion, oil, garlic, pepper, and steak sauce in a saucepan and bring to a boil. Remove from heat and let cool. Put the venison in a covered dish and cover with marinade. Marinate in refrigerator for 1 to 2 hours. Preheat grill to 325°. Put meat on skewers, and add onion or green pepper chunks if desired. Grill for about 2 to 3 minutes per side (cook to medium or medium rare.)

Easy Citrus Kabobs
SERVES 4

Ingredients	Directions
1 pound venison kabob meat, cut into 2-inch cubes ¼ cup freshly squeezed lemon or lime juice 1 lemon, sliced 1 small sweet onion, sliced	Put all ingredients in a Ziploc baggie or covered dish, mix, and marinate in refrigerator for 2 to 4 hours. Preheat grill to 325°. Put meat on skewers and grill for about 2 to 3 minutes per side (cook to medium or medium rare.) While the meat is cooking, sauté the onion slices in olive oil. Serve with rice as a side.

Southwest Kabobs

SERVES 4

Ingredients	Directions
1 pound venison kabob meat, cut into 2-inch cubes	Put venison in covered dish, cover with marinade, and marinate in refrigerator for ½ hour. Thread meat onto skewers. Preheat grill to 325°. Lightly coat grill with nonstick cooking spray, heat, and grill about 5 minutes. The meat should be just getting firm to the touch—you want these medium rare.

Cilantro-Lime Marinade

Ingredients	Directions
½ cup freshly squeezed lime juice 2 tablespoons olive oil 4 medium cloves garlic, minced 8 tablespoons chopped fresh cilantro 1 to 2 teaspoons chili powder 1 to 2 teaspoons cumin 1 teaspoon salt	Place the lime juice, olive oil, garlic, cilantro, chili powder, cumin, and salt in a closed jar and shake until well mixed.

Scrumptious Chops

SERVES 4

Ingredients	Directions
4 boneless center cut venison chops, 1-inch thick Salt and freshly ground black pepper 4 tablespoons unsalted butter 1 medium onion, finely chopped 5 shallots, finely chopped 2 cloves garlic, chopped 1 cup red wine ½ cup heavy cream	Preheat oven to 200°. Season chops with salt and pepper. Heat skillet on medium high. Melt 2 tablespoons of the butter in the pan. Pan sear the chops for about 4 minutes, until the outside is golden brown, then turn over and continue cooking for another 4 minutes. Remove chops from pan and put in warm oven. Add the onion to the skillet (add more butter if pan looks too dry) and cook until browned. Add the shallots and garlic and cook for 1 minute. Pour red wine into pan and bring to boil. Turn the heat down to simmer, and cook until the wine is reduced by half (about 3 to 4 minutes). Add the remaining butter, stirring to melt. Whisk in the cream. Season with additional salt and pepper. Return the chops to the pan and heat for 2 to 4 minutes, until the chops are slightly firm to the touch. Serve immediately.

Rack of Venison with Shallots and Garlic

SERVES 4

Ingredients	Directions
2 tablespoons whole grain mustard	Whisk together mustard, honey, and lemon juice until well blended. Pierce venison all over with tip of small knife or sharp fork. Spoon the mustard mix over meat, making sure to rub it into the pierced areas. Set in pan, cover, and refrigerate for 2 hours.
2 tablespoons honey	
Juice of 1 lemon	
1 (3- to 4-pound) rack of venison	
Salt and pepper to taste	
12 shallots, peeled	
12 cloves garlic, peeled	Preheat oven to 300°.
1 tablespoon olive oil	Place venison, meat side up, on a rack in the roasting pan. Surround with shallots and garlic and drizzle them with the olive oil. Roast 45 minutes to 1 hour, basting every 10 minutes, until the internal temperature reaches 125°. Let the meat sit until the internal temperature reaches 135° (rare) or 145° (medium). This is a dish that must be served medium to medium rare—it will be awful otherwise.
	Slice and spoon shallots and garlic over each piece.

Saffron Rack

SERVES 4

Ingredients	Directions
½ cup Spanish olive oil	Preheat oven to 300°.
2 large cloves garlic, minced	Mix all ingredients, except venison, together. Rub meat with mixture and place in roasting pan. Cook covered until meat's internal temperature is 125° (about 1 hour). Remove from oven and let the meat sit until the internal temperature reaches 135° (rare) or 145° (medium). Serve with saffron rice.
½ teaspoon coriander	
½ teaspoon cumin	
½ teaspoon sea salt	
½ teaspoon saffron, crumbled	
1 rack of venison, Frenched (instructions, page 10)	

Jalapeno Stuffed Tenderloin

SERVES 2 TO 4

Ingredients	Directions
1 (12-ounce) butterflied venison tenderloin/ backstrap (instructions, page 10)	Pour marinade over meat and refrigerate for 20 to 45 minutes.
1 cup chipotle lime marinade (found in the BBQ aisle of the store)	Mix the cream cheese and garlic well. Fill the peppers with the cream cheese mixture. Place the peppers inside the meat, fold the meat over, and then wrap the entire backstrap with the bacon, securing each piece with toothpicks.
1 clove garlic, minced	
½ cup cream cheese, softened	
2 medium jalapenos, de-seeded and halved lengthwise	
Low-sodium bacon (about 8 strips)	Preheat grill to 350°.
2 tablespoons honey	Mix the honey, water, and crushed black pepper. Put the mixture in a small sauce pan and heat on the stove. Set aside.
2 tablespoons water	
1 teaspoon crushed black peppercorns	

Heat a skillet on medium high, and brown the meat on each side for one minute, brushing with the honey paste. Remove from skillet and transfer to grill. Grill until the meat reaches 125° inside (about 10 minutes per side, depending on how thick the meat is). Remove from grill and let the meat sit until the internal temperature reaches 135° (rare) or 145° (medium). Slice into 2 to 3 inch slices and serve.

Venison Potato Roll

SERVES 2 TO 4

Ingredients	Directions
1 (12-ounce) venison tenderloin/backstrap, butterflied (instructions, page 10) 2 tablespoons fresh sage, chopped 5 slices hickory smoked bacon	Preheat oven or grill to 350°. Place the meat on a cutting board. Spread a ¼-inch layer of the potatoes over the meat (if you make the layer too thick, the meat won't roll up). Sprinkle the sage on the potatoes. Roll the meat. Spread slices of bacon in a row on a cutting board. Place the meat roll on the bacon, then wrap each slice around the meat and secure it with toothpicks. Heat a skillet on medium high and brown the meat roll on each side for about 1 minute. If cooking in the oven, transfer to a baking pan; if grilling, place directly on the grill. In both cases, cook each side for about 10 minutes, until the internal temperature reaches 125°. Let sit until internal temperature reaches 135° (rare) to 145° (medium). Slice in 2- to 3-inch slices and serve with extra potatoes on the side.

Mashed Red Potatoes

Ingredients	Directions
Baby red potatoes Butter Cream Salt and pepper	Boil the potatoes, skin on, until tender. Place in a bowl and add butter and cream. Mash with a masher until creamy. Add more butter and/or cream as needed. Add salt and pepper to taste.

Smoked BBQ Venison

SERVES 8

Ingredients	Directions
1 (2-pound) venison roast	Marinate roast in refrigerator in water and liquid smoke for 20 minutes.
5 tablespoons liquid smoke	
2 cups water	Smoke the roast, either using your smoker or your gas grill (instructions, page 10). Remove from smoker when the meat reaches an internal temperature of 135°, which should take about 3 hours for a 2-pound roast. Pull the meat off the bone and chop finely. Coat with BBQ sauce; the amount depends on how saucy you like your meat.
1 to 2 jars of BBQ sauce (your favorite brand)	

Serve with coleslaw and potato salad.

Jaeger Schnitzel

SERVES 8

Ingredients	Directions

Ingredients

1 cup flour

1 teaspoon salt

¼ teaspoon freshly ground black pepper

2 eggs, lightly beaten

4 tablespoons milk

2 cups dry bread crumbs

1 cup crushed buttery cracker crumbs

2 pounds venison flank steak, butterflied (instructions, page 10)

1 cup cooking oil

½ onion, finely chopped

1 to 2 cups mushrooms, sliced

½ cup sherry

½ cup venison stock (page 11) or beef broth

½ cup cream

½ bunch parsley, chopped

Directions

In a large shallow dish, combine flour, salt, and pepper. Dredge the meat in the seasoned flour. Place on a cutting board and cover with wax paper. Using a meat mallet, pound it down to just slightly less than its ¼-inch thickness (the meat may tear a bit…that's the problem with very lean meat). In another shallow bowl, combine eggs and milk. In a third shallow dish, combine bread crumbs and cracker crumbs.

Preheat the oil in a large heavy skillet over medium high heat. Dip the meat in the egg mixture and then coat each piece on both sides with the crumbs. Place the pieces gently in a single layer into the hot oil. Fry the meat for 3 to 4 minutes on each side, or until golden brown. Drain on paper towels, then place on a plate in a warm oven while preparing the sauce.

Using the skillet you used for the meat, fry the chopped onion and mushrooms for a couple of minutes (add or remove oil as needed so that there is about 1 tablespoon of oil in the skillet). Add the sherry to the pan and bring to a boil, then add the broth. Reduce heat and simmer until sauce is reduced to your desired consistency. Remove skillet from heat and slowly stir in the cream. Add the parsley. Ladle sauce over meat and serve the dish with thinly cut french fries (that's the way Rick ate it in Germany).

Taqueria Style Venison Tacos

SERVES 3 TO 4

Ingredients	Directions
1½ pounds venison flank steak	Lay the flank steak in a large dish.
3 tablespoons white wine vinegar	In a medium bowl, whisk together the vinegar, Worcestershire sauce, water, garlic, lime juice, and olive oil. Add the salt, black pepper, white pepper, garlic powder, chili powder, oregano, cumin, and paprika and whisk until well blended. Pour mixture over the meat. Turn the meat over once to coat both sides. Cover with plastic wrap, and marinate refrigerated for 1 to 4 hours.
4 tablespoons Worcestershire sauce	
1 tablespoon water	
2 cloves garlic, minced	
Juice of 1 lime	
¼ cup olive oil	
½ teaspoon salt	
½ teaspoon freshly ground black pepper	
½ teaspoon ground white pepper	Make the onion relish and roasted vegetable salsa (next page) and set aside
½ teaspoon garlic powder	
½ teaspoon chili powder	
½ teaspoon dried oregano	Heat vegetable oil in a large skillet over medium-high heat. Cut the marinated venison into cubes or strips. Cook, stirring constantly, until the meat is cooked through and most of the liquid has evaporated.
½ teaspoon ground cumin	
½ teaspoon paprika	
Onion Relish	
Roasted Vegetable Salsa	Arrange 2 or 3 tortillas on a plate, and lay a generous amount of venison over them. Top with a sprinkle of the onion relish and a large spoonful of the pureed salsa. Add as much cheese as you like. Garnish with lime wedges, and serve.
8 soft corn tortillas (warmed*)	
1 cup grated Cheddar cheese (optional)	
1 lime, cut into wedges	

When you are done roasting the vegetables, turn off the oven, wrap the tortillas in foil and place in the oven while preparing the meat.

Onion Relish
SERVES 3 TO 4

Ingredients	Directions
½ white onion, chopped ¼ cup chopped fresh cilantro Juice of ½ lime	In a small bowl, mix together onion, cilantro, and lime juice.

Roasted Vegetable Salsa
SERVES 3 TO 4

Ingredients	Directions
2 dried New Mexico chile pods 1 large tomato, chopped ½ white onion, quartered 1 jalapeno pepper, chopped 2 cloves garlic, peeled ½ pinch salt and pepper to taste	Heat a skillet over medium-high heat. Toast chile pods in the skillet for a few minutes, then place in a bowl of water to soak for about 30 minutes. Preheat oven to 450°. Place tomato, onion, jalapeno, and garlic onto a baking sheet. Roast in the oven for about 20 minutes, until toasted but not burnt. Place the roasted vegetables and soaked chile pods into a blender or food processor, along with salt and pepper. Puree until smooth.

Venison Fajitas
SERVES 6 TO 8

Ingredients	Directions

½ cup olive oil

⅓ cup freshly squeezed lime juice

½ teaspoon salt

¼ teaspoon cumin

3 cloves garlic, minced

¼ cup white wine vinegar

½ cup chopped onion

1 teaspoon oregano

½ teaspoon pepper

½ tablespoon paprika

1 (12-ounce) can light beer

2 pounds venison flank steak

Flour tortillas

1 tablespoon oil

1 large onion, sliced

1 large green pepper, sliced

Guacamole

Sour cream

Cheddar cheese, shredded

Tomatoes, diced

Combine the olive oil, lime juice, salt, cumin, garlic, vinegar, chopped onion, oregano, pepper, paprika, and beer and mix well. Place the meat in a baking dish and cover with the marinade. Turn meat over to make sure both sides are coated. Marinate in refrigerator for 2 to 5 hours.

Heat the oven to warm. Wrap the flour tortillas in foil and place in oven.

Remove the meat from marinade and slice into long thin strips (about ½-inch wide and ⅓-inch thick). Set aside.

Heat oil in heavy skillet on high. Sauté onion and pepper until the onion is translucent, about 5 minutes. Reduce heat to medium and add meat. Cook until meat is rare (the outsides are brown, but the meat is springy to the touch). Place the meat, onions, and peppers in a bowl or serve in the skillet.

Serve immediately over tortillas and garnish with guacamole, sour cream, cheese, and tomatoes.

Otherwise known as "lunch," sandwiches and salads are a great thing to do with your venison leftovers. Both have been around for almost as long as people have been eating. Sandwiches date back to the 1st century B.C. and a famous rabbi, Hillel the Elder, who began the Passover custom of sandwiching a mixture of chopped nuts, apples, spices, and wine between two matzohs to eat with bitter herbs. However, John Montagu, the Fourth Earl of Sandwich, made them famous. Legend has it that he refused to leave the gambling tables to eat, and rather would have his valets bring him bread with meat stuffed in it.

Sandwiches are great, but I think salad is one of the most versatile foods. Ask someone to bring a salad to the picnic, and you could end up with a 3-bean salad, potato salad, jello, or leafy green salad. Salad dates back to the Greek and Roman times. Today, main course salads are a staple of many diets, but you either love them or don't—my husband claims they are "food that food eats." I disagree. My day wouldn't be complete without a tasty salad topped with grilled venison for lunch! For the purposes of this cookbook, salad means the leafy green variety or the meat-mixed-with-mayonnaise type of salads.

Typically, we use leftovers from roasts or steaks for these dishes. However, that should not stop you from cooking up some meat specifically for these delicious meals.

Venison Reuben Sandwich

SERVES I

Ingredients	Directions
2 slices rye bread Thousand Island dressing (recipe below) 2 slices Swiss cheese ¼ cup sauerkraut Thinly sliced Corned Venison (recipe, page 75) Butter	Spread the Thousand Island dressing on each slice of bread. Layer a slice of the cheese on top of the dressing. Layer the sauerkraut on top of the cheese. Layer the Corned Venison on one slice of bread and put the other slice of bread (cheese side down) on top. Heat a griddle or frying pan on the stove. Spread butter on the outsides of the bread. Place on the griddle and grill until bread is toasted and cheese has melted.

Homemade Thousand Island Dressing

Ingredients	Directions
½ cup mayonnaise ½ cup ketchup ⅛ cup sweet pickle relish 1 teaspoon Worcestershire sauce	Mix all ingredients in a small bowl and refrigerate for at least 2 hours before serving (preferably overnight).

Roast Venison Sandwich

SERVES 1

Ingredients	Directions
1/2 teaspoon brown mustard 1/4 teaspoon horseradish 2 slices rye bread 3 ounces Salt Roast, thinly sliced (recipe, page 69) 2 ounces Brie, sliced	Spread mustard and horseradish on bread. Layer on the meat and cheese. Top with the other slice of bread and cut in half on the diagonal.

Avocado and Roast Sandwich

SERVES 1

Ingredients	Directions
2 slices sourdough bread 1 tablespoon mayonnaise 3 ounces Salt Roast, thinly sliced (recipe, page 69) 2 ounces Havarti cheese, sliced 3 thin slices avocado 1 slice tomato 1 leaf baby romaine lettuce	Toast bread. Spread mayonnaise on one slice, then layer with roast, cheese, avocado, tomato, and lettuce. Top with other slice of bread and cut in half on the diagonal.

Venison and Artichoke Salad Sandwich

SERVES 1

Ingredients	Directions
½ pound venison, cut into small cubes 1 teaspoon olive oil 4 canned artichoke hearts, chopped 1 tablespoon capers 1 tablespoon mayonnaise 1 teaspoon tarragon Salt to taste 2 slices of hearty, whole grain bread	Sauté the venison cubes in the olive oil until medium rare (just a few minutes of cooking). Let cool. Put in a bowl with artichoke hearts, capers, mayonnaise, and tarragon and mix well. Add salt to taste. Spread on one slice of bread and cover with other slice. Cut along the diagonal.

Venison Spinach and Pasta Salad

SERVES 4

Ingredients	Directions
1 pound venison flank steak or backstrap	Preheat grill to 300°.
Olive oil	Rub the venison with olive oil and grill until the meat is rare (about 4 minutes per side, depending on how thick the meat is). Remove from grill and cool.
2 cups cooked bow tie pasta, cooled	
1 (6-ounce) bag baby spinach	
1 large ripe tomato, chopped	
1 cup sliced halved cucumbers	Slice the meat into thin, bite-size strips.
1 cup feta cheese, crumbled	Toss pasta with spinach, venison, tomato, cucumber, and ½ cup of the cheese in a large bowl. Add dressing; mix lightly.
½ cup of your favorite vinaigrette	Sprinkle with remaining ½ cup cheese.

Rotini with Basil, Tomato, and Venison

SERVES 2

Ingredients	Directions
1 (16-ounce) package rotini pasta	Prepare pasta according to package directions. Preheat grill to 300°. Rub the backstrap with olive oil and grill until the meat is rare (about 4 minutes per side, depending on how thick the backstrap is). Remove from grill and cool. Cut into bite-size pieces.
½ pound venison backstrap	
1 tablespoon olive oil	
1 tablespoon red wine vinegar	
¼ cup freshly grated Parmesan cheese	
¼ cup chopped fresh basil	
1 medium tomato, chopped	Toss pasta with oil, vinegar and cheese. Add venison, basil, and tomato. Season with salt and ground black pepper.
Salt and ground black pepper to taste	

Venison and Wild Rice Salad

SERVES 6 TO 8

Ingredients	*Directions*
½ cup walnuts	In a dry skillet, toast walnuts over medium to high heat for 1 minute or until lightly browned. Set aside.
2 cups water	
½ teaspoon salt	
1 cup brown and wild rice blend	In a medium saucepan, bring water and salt to boil. Add rice, stir well, cover, and reduce heat to simmer. Cook for 40 to 45 minutes, or until rice is tender and all water has been absorbed. Remove from heat. Let stand 10 minutes.
½ pound venison backstrap	
1 garlic clove, minced	
1 teaspoon minced orange zest	
2 teaspoons coarse Dijon mustard	Heat the grill to 300°. Rub the backstrap with olive oil and grill until the meat is rare (about 5 minutes per side, depending on how thick the backstrap is). Remove from grill and cool. Cut into bite-size pieces.
2 tablespoon orange juice concentrate	
¼ cup sherry vinegar	
½ cup olive oil	
½ teaspoon salt	
½ cup dried cranberries	In a small bowl, combine garlic, orange zest, and mustard; blend well. Whisk in orange juice concentrate and vinegar. Slowly whisk in oil and salt.
½ red pepper, thinly sliced	
3 scallions, thinly sliced	

Transfer cooked rice to large bowl. Add half the orange mixture and toss gently to coat well. Cool to room temperature. Add walnuts, venison, cranberries, red pepper, and scallions just before serving. Toss. Add remaining dressing to lightly coat vegetables. Toss again and serve.

Steak Salad with Cranberry Dressing
SERVES 4

Ingredients	Directions
1 pound venison flank steak or backstrap	Preheat grill to 300°.
2 tablespoons olive oil	Rub the venison with olive oil and grill until the meat is rare (about 5 minutes per side, depending on how thick the meat is). Remove from grill and cool. Slice the meat into thin, bite-size strips.
8 cups mixed salad greens	
10 cherry tomatoes, halved	
¼ cup Gorgonzola, crumbled	
¼ cup walnuts, chopped (optional)	
½ red onion, thinly sliced	Place 2 cups of greens on a plate. Sprinkle with tomatoes, Gorgonzola, walnuts, and onion. Add strips of meat and drizzle with a tablespoon of salad dressing. Set the extra dressing on the table in case anyone wants more!
Cranberry Dressing	

Cranberry Dressing

Ingredients	Directions
3 tablespoons red wine vinegar	In a blender or food processor, combine vinegar, oil, cranberries, mustard, garlic, salt, pepper, and water; blend or process until smooth.
⅓ cup extra-virgin olive oil	
¼ cup cranberries (if frozen, thaw)	
1 tablespoon Dijon mustard	NOTE: *This is a very thick dressing.*
½ teaspoon minced garlic	
¼ teaspoon salt	
¼ teaspoon pepper	
1 tablespoon water	

Arugula and Blue Cheese Salad with Venison

SERVES 4

Ingredients	Directions
1 pound venison flank steak	Preheat grill to 300°. Brush the meat with olive oil and grill until it's medium rare. Slice into strips and set aside to cool.
1 tablespoon olive oil	
1 teaspoon Dijon mustard	
¼ cup red wine vinegar	In a bowl whisk together mustard, vinegar, and salt and pepper to taste. Slowly whisk in the oil, dribbling it in a slow stream.
Salt and pepper to taste	
⅓ cup olive oil	
6 cups arugula, washed and dried	In a large bowl, toss the arugula, blue cheese, and cranberries with enough of the dressing to just coat the leaves. Put the salad mixture on a plate and top with grilled venison. Serve with a nice sourdough bread.
¼ pound blue cheese, coarsely crumbled	
⅓ cup dried cranberries	

Grilled Venison Salad with Tangy Lemon Dressing

SERVES 4

	Directions
1 pound venison tenderloin or kabob meat	
2 tablespoons olive oil	Preheat grill to 300°. Brush the meat with olive oil and grill until it's medium rare (time will depend on how thick the meat is). Slice into strips and set aside to cool.
8 cups loosely packed baby spinach	
2 tomatoes, cut in wedges	
1 yellow pepper, sliced	
	Toss spinach with dressing. Put on plate and garnish with tomato, yellow pepper, and venison.

Tangy Lemon Dressing

Ingredients	Directions
Juice of 4 lemons	In a blender or mini food processor, pulse lemon juice, oil, walnuts, mustard, and salt until smooth.
4 tablespoons olive oil	
6 tablespoons walnuts	
4 teaspoons Dijon mustard	
1 teaspoon sea salt	

Spinach Salad with Grilled Venison Tenderloin

SERVES 4

Ingredients	Directions
8 cups baby spinach	Wash the spinach, dry, and set aside. Wash the mushrooms, dry, remove stems, and slice thinly. On each plate, put 2 cups of spinach topped with the mushrooms, olives, Feta, and venison strips. Toss with Balsamic vinaigrette. Serve with a crusty French bread.
½ cup white mushrooms	
¼ cup olives (mixture of green and black)	
½ cup Feta cheese, crumbled	
12 ounces grilled venison medallions (recipe on page 79), sliced into strips	
Balsamic vinaigrette	

Balsamic Vinaigrette

Ingredients	Directions
⅓ cup olive oil	Put all ingredients in a covered container and mix well. Recipe makes about 1 cup, and will last in the refrigerator for about 1 week
2 tablespoons balsamic vinegar	
2 tablespoons apple cider vinegar	
2 teaspoons Dijon mustard	
1 clove garlic, crushed	
Salt and pepper to taste	

Mexican Chef Salad
SERVES 4 TO 6

Ingredients	Directions
1 large package of mixed greens 2 tomatoes, chopped ½ small red onion, sliced 1 cup sharp Cheddar cheese, grated ½ pound ground venison, browned Mexican Thousand Island Dressing	Mix greens, tomatoes, sliced onion, cheese, and venison in a bowl, and toss with about ½ cup of Mexican Thousand Island Dressing. Put the remaining dressing in a bowl for those who may want more. Serve salad with tortilla chips.

Mexican Thousand Island Dressing

Ingredients	Directions
¼ cup mayonnaise ½ stalk celery, chopped very fine ¼ small red onion, chopped very fine 1 tablespoon chili sauce 1 hard-boiled egg, chopped	For the dressing, mix the mayonnaise, celery, red onion, chili sauce, and egg together. Let refrigerate for 1 day before serving. This recipe yields about 1 cup.

Southwest Venison Salad
SERVES 4

Ingredients	Directions
Nonstick cooking spray 1 pound venison flank steak 1 (15-ounce) can black beans, drained 4 medium to large Roma tomatoes, diced 8 tablespoons chopped scallions 4 cups romaine lettuce Cilantro-Lime Marinade (recipe page 83)	Lightly coat a grill with nonstick cooking spray, preheat to 325°, and grill the venison until done. Slice into 1-inch strips. Mix together the venison, beans, tomatoes, scallions, lettuce, and dressing, and serve with tortilla chips.

Chipotle Ranch Salad

SERVES 4

Ingredients

¼ cup fresh salsa

3 tablespoons fresh cilantro leaves

1 clove garlic

1 cup ranch dressing

¼ teaspoon ground Chipotle Chile Powder OR 2 teaspoons Chipotle Sauce

1 pound venison flank steak, cut into strips

Olive oil

Salt and pepper to taste

1 head romaine lettuce

Cherry tomatoes

Cheddar cheese, grated

Red onion, sliced

Directions

For the dressing, put salsa, cilantro, and garlic in food processor and pulse until finely chopped. Add ranch dressing and Chipotle powder or sauce, and process until well combined. This recipe yields about 1½ cups, and it will keep in the refrigerator for a few weeks.

Preheat grill to 300°. Slice the venison into 1-inch strips. Rub with oil, salt and pepper. Grill until medium rare (about 2 minutes per side). Remove from grill and set aside.

Wash the romaine well, dry with paper towel, and tear leaves into bite-size pieces. Put lettuce, tomatoes, cheese, and onion in a bowl and toss with dressing until lettuce is well coated. Transfer to a dinner plate and top with the grilled venison. Serve with tortilla chips.

Venison Chef Salad

SERVES 4 TO 6

Ingredients

½ pound venison flank steak

Olive oil

½ cup apple preserves

½ cup vegetable oil

¼ cup freshly squeezed lemon juice

½ teaspoon garlic salt

6 cups torn mixed salad greens

4 hard-boiled eggs, sliced

1 cup grated sharp Cheddar cheese

1 tomato, sliced into wedges

½ cucumber, peeled and sliced

Directions

Preheat grill to 300°. Brush the meat with olive oil and grill until it's medium rare (time will depend on how thick the meat is). Slice into strips and set aside to cool.

In a blender or food processor, combine preserves, oil, lemon juice, and garlic salt; chill. In a large salad bowl, combine remaining ingredients with dressing; toss lightly. Serve with a crusty French bread and butter.

One of the biggest barriers to convincing your family and friends that they want to eat venison is the bad reputation it has for being tough and gamey. The truth is, venison is delicious when it is prepared right, and terrible when done wrong. Preparing venison right starts in the field with the hunter. Although this is a cookbook, proper harvesting is so critical to producing good-tasting meat that I think a tutorial on harvesting is important. This tutorial is courtesy of my hunter, Rick, who has a stellar reputation for harvesting the most delicious meat you will ever eat.

The key elements to producing good meat for the table are:
- Cooling the meat as quickly as possible,
- Keeping the meat clean,
- Aging it properly, and
- Packaging and freezing well.

If you think about it in comparison to how beef is processed, these steps make sense: Beef cows (not bulls) are walked up a chute into an abattoir where they're quickly dispatched. The cow is then immediately taken to a climate-controlled room and gutted and skinned to cool quickly. The two sides of beef are split from each other and hung to age in a perfectly controlled, low-humidity, 40° cooler for a few days to weeks, depending on the grade of beef. Once the beef has aged appropriately, it is quartered and broken down into the cuts for the consumer. It's often shipped in a partially frozen state to be further processed at the supermarkets or butcher and packaged there. At the store, beef frequently has either carbon monoxide or additives applied to keep it looking "fresh". At every step, there are quality control measures in place to make sure the meat always tastes good.

The methods for deer are different, but the general process is the same. If you keep quality in mind, you'll have a good outcome.

THE CHALLENGES OF HARVESTING VENISON

Chances are, you don't have climate-controlled harvesting conditions in the field, commercial freezers at home, or butchers willing to stay open late so you can deliver your deer when you come out of the woods. But these factors impact how good the meat tastes.

Also, many hunters are looking for that trophy buck. When they get a chance to shoot one, they let the animal sit for an extended time to make sure it expires—nothing is worse than the thought of losing that trophy. Most hunters are taught that it's better to come back the next day if they're unsure about the shot. That works out fine if all you want from the deer are antlers, but it doesn't work out well for the quality of the meat.

HOW TO PROPERLY HARVEST DEER

If you're hunting to put good food on your family's table, here is the right way to harvest deer.

Make absolutely sure when you take the shot it will be a quick kill and easy recovery. If it's warm out and you're confident in your shot, wait 15 to 30 minutes to retrieve. If it's really cold out, you can wait longer. Quickly find your deer. It helps to hunt with a buddy so all the steps following the kill go faster. Remember, you want to cool the meat as quickly as possible. Once you find the animal, think about how you're going to get it to a vehicle. If you crossed streams or muddy bogs to find it, drag the deer back closer to the vehicle before gutting it. This keeps water and mud from entering the shot holes and into the deer, and keeping the meat clean and sanitary is important.

FIELD DRESSING THE DEER

Everybody has their own way of doing this, but this is Rick's method. After using this method to harvest many deer (sometimes two or three in one day), he has found this to be quick and easy, and it keeps the meat from getting contaminated.

Your Knife

All you need is a 3- to 4-inch blade. It doesn't need to be the most expensive knife out there; what it needs to be is extremely sharp (sharp enough to shave with). A slight curve back at the end bit with a good point is Rick's favorite. It's easy to control, the tip pierces through the hide easily, and with the slight curve it cuts through the hide well without diving into the gut (extremely important for tasty meat).

STEP 1: When you find your animal, make sure it's dead. The eyes should be open, and if you stick you gun muzzle or arrow to an eyeball and touch it, the animal should not blink.

STEP 2: Position the animal on its back. Cut the anus and vagina free from the outside and interior pelvis. Insert the knife between the tail and the anus. When putting the knife in, try to keep the point angled into the bones of the pelvis and not into the pelvic cavity. Cut a hole around the anus and vagina (if it's a doe). Once you have cut all the way around, stick your fingers into the cut and try to separate the intestines and vagina from the wall of the pelvis; this is all held together by some thin connective membranes. If you need to use your knife, do so carefully. You don't want to cut the urine bladder or tube. Once you think it's pretty free, cut up to the chest bone.

STEP 3: Make an incision through the hide down to the breast plate, starting at the top of the breastbone (sternum). Continue the incision to the soft spot just below the sternum. Carefully puncture through the hide here, but without puncturing the stomach. You can lift the hide below the puncture area to help keep the knife from hitting the stomach.

Take the knife out and stick two fingers of your non-knife hand into the incision and lift the hide away from the abdominal organs.

Using your fingers as a guide, put the knife between them and run an incision down to the pubic bone. Your fingers will be pulling the hide up and away, allowing the knife to just slide down the hide. Be careful of your fingers! Don't cut the hide past the pubic bone; if you do it will pull up the legs exposing the meat to possible contamination. If this happens, you just need to more careful about keeping that meat clean.

STEP 4: The next step is to cut the sternum. Depending on the deer's size, you can either cut through the sternum to open the chest or cut the ribs free on one side of the sternum. Small deer can be cut through the bone. Use a pulling motion to achieve this. It is counter to what you are taught about cutting away from you, but you can control your knife better and not have it twist and accidentally cut something you don't want cut.

Now, standing over the deer, face the tail and put the knife either along the side of the sternum or right at the bottom, depending on whether you plan to cut the ribs or the bone. Using the weight of the deer, pull toward the head and slice up to the top of the sternum. It may take a couple of pulls.

STEP 5: Now you are ready to remove the insides. The organs are anchored in place by a connective tissue membrane, the esophagus and windpipe, and the diaphragm muscle. After you cut these free, you will dump them out to one side. You are first going to cut free the diaphragm on whichever side will eventually be down when you dump.

The thin muscle between the chest and the abdomen is the diaphragm. While the deer is still on its back, cut the diaphragm free from one side starting at the middle and working down to the backbone. You may need to tilt the deer slightly. Pull the organs away from the knife while you cut. Then cut the lungs free from that same side, working along the inside of the ribs. They should fall away easily. Repeat on the other side as much as possible.

Reach into the neck and find the windpipe and esophagus. Slip your fingers under them pushing through the connective tissue that holds them to the backbone. Once you have a good hold of them, you cut them off above your hand. Holding firmly, you should be able to pull them back toward the tail. You may need to free part of the lungs with your knife, but Rick finds a good steady pull works fine. Let the deer fall to the side you cut free earlier, pulling the chest organs out. The abdominal organs should follow, but you may have to free them from the back wall with a knife as you pull. You should be able to pull everything free all the way to the pelvis.

To remove the bladder and intestines from the pelvis, reach into the pelvis, grab the intestines at the very end, and pull out. Don't squeeze the bladder. If you cut the bladder and intestines free earlier (see Step 2) they'll just pull out. If they aren't coming loose, carefully use your knife to scrape along the inside walls and free up the membrane holding them in and try again.

Everything should be out now. Rick likes to cut out the heart and liver to make treats for our dog (she likes that too). If you take the liver, put it in a separate container from any other meat. Rick keeps a Ziploc bag with his gear just for that.

STEP 6: Turn the dear over on its belly, and put the head back on its shoulders. This will drain most of the blood out. While that's draining, clean up and put away your dressing equipment.

Now you need to get your deer out of the woods.

How to Get the Deer Out of the Woods

After you're done field dressing your deer, you have to get it out of the woods. This is the hardest part of the day. It helps to have a Sherpa or teenage boys on hand at this point, but most often you're on your own.

Depending on terrain, weather, and so on, you may choose to get the deer out any number of ways. If getting a vehicle close is an option, Rick will flip the deer back over, put a clean stick between the halves of the chest and open it up to allow air circulation, then go get the truck, bringing everything with him except the deer. If the vehicle is close enough, his buddy and he pick the deer up by the legs and carry it to the truck.

If he has to drag the deer out of the woods, then he ties the front legs together with a piece of string and makes a cut through both lower legs just above the hooves between the Achilles tendon and the leg bone. He passes his drag rope through these cuts and pulls the deer by the rear legs. This method tends to keep the meat away from the dirt while dragging. And if it's a buck, the antlers are less likely to catch things when dragged backwards.

The ultimate tool, however, is the deer cart. The deer stays out of the dirt and it is much easier to transport through the woods. The exception to this is stream crossings or deep snow.

Transporting the Deer

Once back at the truck, ice the deer as soon as possible. Rick carries a cooler with bagged ice whenever he goes hunting any distance from home. Place the bag of ice in the body cavity of the deer for the trip home. If it's a big deer, stop as soon as you can for a couple more bags of ice. If you're in a warm climate, throw a couple bags on top of the deer as well.

If you're taking your deer to a processor, you're done with your part. If you have to wait for the processor to open, keep cooling the deer with the ice.

Processing the Deer

Most hunters take their meat to a processor, who will do an excellent job of making sure the cuts are prepared well. Rick and many of his hunting buddies process the meat themselves, which he prefers. If you want to learn how to do that, visit our website (greatvenisioncooking.com) for diagrams and tutorials on how to process the meat.

ACKNOWLEDGEMENTS

I want to thank everyone who has sampled my venison dishes, shared family recipes, and put up with me talking nonstop about marinades and meat grinders for the past few years. I especially want to thank Rick for introducing me to venison (and for generally being a great guy and terrific husband). Who knew I would find such a passion for cooking this meat the first time he asked me to try it?

Special thanks go to my talented sister Karen Loehr for designing this beautiful book and my equally talented sister-in-law Peggy for shooting the cover and the pictures of me cooking, Susan Trivers for reading the first draft, and Dan Loehr, Monica Parham, and Nina Seebeck for editing and proofreading (both of which I really need and appreciate).

I also want to thank my fabulous braintrust (Joan Fletcher, Kelly O'Brien, and Susan Trivers) who supported me throughout. Thanks to my sister-in-law Lynn for letting me use her beautiful kitchen for the photo shoots.

For the photo shoot, I had my makeup done by Mary Kay Independent Beauty Consultant Monica Mayk Parham. If you like the look and want to try it out, try the virtual makeover at www.marykay.com/monicaparham.

RESOURCES

On-line Venison Suppliers

If the freezer starts to run low, no worries. There are many venison (and other game suppliers) online who can ship your venison to you. The following is a partial list of suppliers.

Broken Arrow Ranch
http://brokenarrowranch.com

Highbourne Deer Farms
http://www.highbourne.com/
(Highbourne Deer Farms' USDA inspected locally raised and produced venison)

iGourmet.com
http://www.igourmet.com/game-meat.asp

Local Harvest
http://www.localharvest.org/venison.jsp

MansMeat.com
http://www.mansmeat.com/meats/venison.htm

Underhill Farms
http://www.underhillfarms.com/products/venison-products.html

Cooking Resources and Tips

These are great resources for more information on how to handle venison or for tutorials on different cooking methods.

Ask the Meat Man
askthemeatman.com

Culinary Institute of America, Online
http://www.ciaprochef.com/

PBS Lessons with Master Chef Julia Child
http://www.pbs.org/juliachild/

Rouxbe Online Cooking School
http://rouxbe.com/cooking-school

Simply Canning
simplycanning.com/index.html

Southern Indian Butcher Supply
butchersupply.net

A

Aging Meat 6

AMERICAN
Appalachian Meat Loaf 62
Apple Rotisserie Roast 72
Asiago Sandwiches 26
BBQ Venison Burger 57
BBQ Venison Meatballs 22
Berry Bacon Pinwheel 24
Buffalo Venison Tenders 28
Cherry Drops 26
Classic Blue Burger 58
Coffee Chili 35
Garlic and Herb Roast 71
Good Old American Burger 57
Good Old American
Meat Loaf 61
Pepper Pinwheels 23
Pepper & Venison Crostini 25
Salt Roast 69, 74
Savory Southwestern
Venison Pie 17
Simple Oven Roast 70
Smoked BBQ Venison 88
Stuffed Mushroom Caps 22
Three Cheese Pasta
and Venison 54
Traditional Yankee
Pot Roast 77
Twenty Minute Chili 32
Twice-Baked Potatoes 63
Venison and Smoked Gouda
Strata 55
Venison Slow Cooker
Pot Roast 73
Yummy-in-the-Tummy Venison
Pot Pie 64

Andouille Sausage 42, 66
Appalachian Meat Loaf 62

APPETIZER
Asiago Sandwiches 26
BBQ Venison Meatballs 22
Berry Bacon Pinwheel 24
Buffalo Venison Tenders 28
Cherry Drops 26
Hot Seven-Layer Dip 17
Pepper Pinwheels 23
Pepper & Venison Crostini 25
Rillettes of Venison 29
Savory Southwestern Venison
Pie 17
Smoky Venison Quesadillas 20
Southwestern Nachos 19
Steak on a Stick: Teriyaki
Skewers 21
Stuffed Mushroom Caps 22
Venison Con Queso 18
Venison Tenderloin with
Bérnaise Sauce 27

Apple Rotisserie Roast 72
Arugula and Blue Cheese Salad
with Venison 100
Asiago Sandwiches 26

ASIAN
Teriyaki Skewers 21

Avocado and Roast Sandwich 96

B

BACKSTRAP
Grilled Tenderloin
Medallions 79
Rotini with Basil, Tomato, and
Venison 97
Steak Salad with Cranberry
Dressing 99
Venison and Smoked Gouda
Strata 55
Venison and Wild Rice
Salad 98
Venison Potato Roll 87
BBQ Venison Burger 57
BBQ Venison Meatballs 22
Béarnaise Sauce 27
Berry Bacon Pinwheel 24

Balsamic Vinaigrette 101
Blue Cheese Dressing 28

BRITISH
Scottish Mince Pie 53
Traditional Shepherd's Pie 51
Buffalo Venison Tenders 28
Butterflying Meat 10–13

C

CAJUN
Fat Tuesday Jambalaya 42

Canning Meat 7

CASSEROLE
Corn and Venison Casserole 49
Enchiladas 48
Mock Lasagna 45
Scottish Mince Pie 53
Spicy Southwestern Casserole 50
Three Cheese Pasta and Venison 54
Traditional Shepherd's Pie 51
Upside Down Shepherd's Pie 51
Vaquero Pie 52
Venison and Artichoke Alfredo 47
Venison and Smoked Gouda Strata 55
Venison Lasagna 44
Venison Stroganoff 46

Cherry Drops 26

CHILI
Cincinnati Skyline Chili 33
Coffee Chili 35
Twenty Minute Chili 32
Venison Chipotle Chili 31
White Venison Chili 34

Chipotle Ranch Salad 103
Chipotle Venison Roast 73
Cincinnati Skyline Chili 33
Classic Blue Burger 58
Coffee Chili 35

COOKING TECHNIQUES
Braising 9
Broiling 9
Browning Ground Venison 9
Butterflying Meat 10

Butter: Salted or Unsalted 11
Dry Heat Cooking 8
Cooking Burgers 9
Frenching Venison 10
General Cooking Advice 8
Gluten Free 12
Grilling 8
Making Venison Stock 10
Marinating 8
Moist Heat Cooking 8
Pan Frying 9
Roasting 8, 12
Roasting Peppers 12
Stewing 9
Using Your Gas Grill as a Smoker 10

COOKING TOOLS
Mortar and Pestle 12
Rotisserie Grill Attachment 12
Stand Mixer with Meat Grinder and Sausage Stuffer 12

Corned Venison 75
Corn & Venison Casserole 49
Cranberry Dressing 99

D
DRESSING
Balsamic Vinaigrette 101
Blue Cheese Dressing 28
Chipotle Ranch Dressing 103
Cranberry Dressing 99
Homemade Thousand Island Dressing 95
Mexican Thousand Island Dressing 102
Tangy Lemon Dressing 100

E
Easy Citrus Kabobs 82
Enchiladas 48

F
Fat Tuesday Jambalaya 42
Field Dressing Deer 106
Fiesta Venison Chowder 37
Fig and Venison Stew 38

FLANK STEAK 97
Arugula and Blue Cheese Salad with Venison 100
Berry Bacon Pinwheel 24
Chipotle Ranch Salad 103
Jaeger Schnitzel 89
Pepper Pinwheels 23
Steak on a Stick: Teriyaki Skewers 21
Southwest Venison Salad 102
Steak Salad with Cranberry Dressing 99
Taqueria Style Venison Tacos 90
Venison Chef Salad 100
Venison Fajitas 92

Flavorful Venison Breakfast Sausage 67
Freezing Meat 7

FRENCH
Andouille Sausage 66
Béarnaise Sauce 27
Frenching Venison 10
Gigot de Venaison 76
Rillettes of Venison 29
Frenching Venison 10–13

G

Garlic and Herb Roast 71

GERMAN
Jaeger Schnitzel 89
Nurenburg Style Brats 66

Gigot de Venaison 76

Good Old American Burger 57

Good Old American Meat Loaf 61

GREEK
Cincinnati Skyline Chili 33

Grilled Tenderloin Medallions 79

Grilled Venison Salad with Tangy
Lemon Dressing 100

Grinding Meat 7

GROUND VENISON
Appalachian Meatloaf 62
BBQ Venison Burger 57
BBQ Venison Meatballs 22
Browning Ground Venison 9
Cincinnati Skyline Chili 33
Classic Blue Burger 58
Coffee Chili 35
Cooking Burgers 9
Enchiladas 48
Good Old American Burger 57
Good Old American Meatloaf 61
Grinding Meat 7
Horseradish Burgers 60
Hot Seven-Layer Dip 17
Hush Burgers 59
Irish Style Mealoaf 61
Mexicali Meat Loaf 62
Mexican Chef Salad 102
Oat Burgers 60

Scottish Mince Pie 53
Spicy Burgers 58
Stand Mixer with Meat Grinder
and Sausage Stuffer 12
Stuffed Mushroom Caps 22
Twenty Minute Chili 32
Twice-Baked Potatoes 63
Upside Down Shepherd's Pie 51
Venison Calzone 64
Venison Chipotle Chili 31
Venison Con Queso 18
Venison Stroganoff 46

Guinness Pub Stew 36

H

Homemade Thousand Island
Dressing 95

Horseradish Burgers 60

Hot Seven-Layer Dip 17

HUNGARIAN
Venison Stroganoff 46

Hush Burgers 59

I

IRISH
Corned Venison 75
Guinness Pub Stew 36
Irish Style Meat Loaf 61

ITALIAN
Venison Calzone 64
Venison Lasagna 44
Venison Meat Sauce 44, 45, 65

J

Jaeger Schnitzel 89

Jalapeno Stuffed Tenderloin 86

K

KABOB MEAT
Easy Citrus Kabobs 82
Savory Kabobs 82
Southwestern Nachos 19

KID FRIENDLY
Corn and Venison Casserole 49
Enchiladas 48
Flavorful Venison Breakfast
Sausage 67
Good Old American Burger 57
Good Old American
Meat Loaf 61
Irish Style Meat Loaf 61
Mock Lasagna 45
Nurenburg Style Brats 66
Rotisserie Roast with Garlic
Rub 77
Scottish Mince Pie 53
Spicy Southwestern
Casserole 50
Southwestern Nachos 19
Three Cheese Pasta and
Venison 54
Traditional Shepherd's Pie 51
Traditional Yankee Pot
Roast 77
Twice-Baked Potatoes 63
Upside Down Shepherd's Pie 51
Vaquero Pie 52
Venison Lasagna 44
Venison Stroganoff 46

Yummy-in-the-Tummy Venison Pot Pie 64

L

Limey Beer Steak 81

Loin Chops with Cranberry Orange Relish 80

M

MARINADES
Cilantro-Lime Marinade 83
Fajita Marinade 92
Red Wine Marinade 82
Taqueria Marinade 90
Teriyaki Sauce 21

Mexicali Meat Loaf 62

MEXICAN 102
Enchiladas 48
Hot Seven-Layer Dip 17
Taco Soup 37
Venison Con Queso 18
Mexican Chef Salad 102
Mexicali Meatloaf 62
Smokey Venison Quesadillas 20

Mexican Thousand Island Dressing 102

MIDDLE EASTERN
Fig and Venison Stew 38
Savory Kabobs 82
Venison Shorba Soup 39

Mock Lasagna 45

Moist Cooking 8

N

NECK ROAST
Corn and Venison Casserole 49
Stewing 9, 29

NORTH AFRICAN
Tunisian Venison Tagine 40

Nurenburg Style Brats 66

NUTRITION 2
Comparison of Meats 4
Nutritional Chart 3

Nutty Venison Saddle in Bacon 78

O

Oat Burgers 60

P

PASTA
Mock Lasagna 45
Rotini with Basil, Tomato, and Venison 97
Three Cheese Pasta and Venison 54
Venison and Artichoke Alfredo 47
Venison Lasagna 44
Venison Spinach and Pasta Salad 97

Pepper Pinwheels 23

Pepper & Venison Crostini 25

PORK
Andouille Sausage 66
Appalachian Meat Loaf 62
Flavorful Venison Breakfast Sausage 67
Irish Meatloaf 61
Nurenburg Style Brats 66

POTATOES
Mashed Red Potatoes 87
Twice-Baked Potatoes 63
Venison Potato Roll 87

PREPARING MEAT
Aging Meat 6
Freezing Meat 7
Grinding Meat 7
Salting 7
Trimming 6

R

RACK OF VENISON
Rack of Venison with Shallots and Garlic 85
Saffron Rack 85
Rack of Venison with Shallots and Garlic 85

Reindeer with Lingonberry Sauce 74

Rillettes of Venison 29

ROAST
Apple Rotisserie Roast 72
Asiago Sandwiches 26
Avocado and Roast Sandwich 96
Corned Venison 75
Chipotle Venison Roast 73
Garlic and Herb Roast 71
Gigot de Venaison 76
Neck Roast 29
Pepper and Venison Crostini 25
Reindeer with LIngonberry Sauce 74
Rilletes of Venison 29

Roast Venison Sandwich 96

Rotisserie Roast with Garlic Rub 77

Salt Roast 69, 74

Simple Oven Roast 70

Smoked BBQ Venison 88

Smoky Venison Quesadillas 20

Traditional Yankee Pot Roast 77

Venison Slow Cooker Pot Roast 73

Roast Venison Sandwich 96

Rotini with Basil, Tomato, and Venison 97

ROTISSERIE
Apple Rotisserie Roast 72

Rotisserie Grill Attachment 12

Rotisserie Roast with Garlic Rub 77

S

SADDLE
Nutty Venison Saddle in Bacon 78

Saffron Rack 85

Sage Steak 81

Salt Roast 69, 74

SAUCES
Béarnaise Sauce 27

Cranberry Orange Relish 80

LIngonberry Sauce 74

Meat Sauce 65

Onion Relish 90, 91

Roasted Vegetable Salsa 90, 91

Venison Meat Sauce 44, 45, 65

SAUSAGE
Andouille Sausage 66

Flavorful Venison Breakfast Sausage 67

Nurenburg Style Brats 66

Stand Mixer with Meat Grinder and Sausage Stuffer 12

Savory Kabobs 82

Savory Southwestern Venison Pie 17

Scottish Mince Pie 53

Scrumptious Chops 84

SHANK END LEG
Gigot de Venaison 76

SHANK STEAK
Stewing 9

Shoulder Roast 76

Apple Rotisserie Roast 72

Garlic and Herb Roast 71

Reindeer with Lingonberry Sauce 74

Simple Oven Roast 70

Traditional Yankee Pot Roast 77

Simple Oven Roast 70

Slow Cooker 37

Chipotle Venison Roast 73

Fig and Venison Stew 38

Taco Soup 37

Tunisian Venison Tagine 40

Venison Slow Cooker Pot Roast 73

Smoked BBQ Venison 88

Simple Oven Roast 70

Shepherd's Pie 51

Smokey Venison Quesadilla 20

SOUP
Making Venison Stock 10

Taco Soup 37

Venison and Wild Rice Soup 41

Venison Shorba Soup 39

SOUTHWEST
Savory Southwestern Venison Pie 17

Southwestern Nachos 19

Southwest Kabobs 83

Southwest Venison Salad 102

Spicy Burgers 58

Spicy Southwestern Casserole 50

Spinach Salad with Grilled Venison Tenderloin 101

STEAK
Buffalo Venison Tenders 28

Southwestern Nachos 19

Steak Meat

Limey Beer Steak 81

Sage Steak 81

Venison and Artichoke Alfredo 47

Steak on a Stick: Teriyaki Skewers 21

Steak Salad with Cranberry Dressing 99

STEW
Fiesta Venison Chowder 37

Fig and Venison Stew 38

Guinness Pub Stew 36

Stewing 9

Tunisian Venison Tagine 40

White Venison Chili 34

Stuffed Mushroom Caps 22

Stew Meat 41

T

Taco Soup 37

Tangy Lemon Dressing 100

Taqueria Style Venison Tacos 90

TENDERLOIN
  Cherry Drops 26

  Grilled Tenderloin Medallions 79

  Grilled Venison Salad with Tangy Lemon Dressing 99

  Venison Tenderloin with Béarnaise Sauce 27

Teriyaki Sauce 21

TEX-MEX
  Chipotle Venison Roast 73

  Corn and Venison Casserole 49

  Fiesta Venison Chowder 37

  Hot Seven-Layer Dip 17

  Mexicali Meat Loaf 62

  Smoky Venison Quesadillas 20

  Spicy Burgers 58

  Taqueria Style Venison Tacos 90

  Vaquero Pie 52

  Venison Chipotle Chili 31

  Venison Fajitas 92

  White Venison Chili 34

Three Cheese Pasta and Venison 54

Traditional Shepherd's Pie 51

Traditional Yankee Pot Roast 77

Trimming Meat 6

Tunisian Venison Tagine 40

Twenty Minute Chili 32

Twice-Baked Potatoes 63

U

Upside Down Shepherd's Pie 51

V

Vaquero Pie 52

Venison and Artichoke Alfredo 47

Venison and Artichoke Salad Sandwich 96

Venison and Smoked Gouda Strata 55

Venison and Wild Rice Salad 98

Venison and Wild Rice Soup 41

Venison Calzone 64

Venison Chef Salad 102

Venison Chipotle Chili 31

Venison Chops

Scrumptious Chops 84

Venison Con Queso 18

Venison Fajitas 92

Venison Lasagna 44

Venison Meat Sauce 44, 45, 65

Venison Potato Roll 87

Venison Reuben Sandwich 95

Venison Shorba Soup 39

Venison Slow Cooker Pot Roast 73

Venison Spinach and Pasta Salad 97

Venison Tenderloin with Béarnaise Sauce 27

W

White Venison Chili 34

Y

Yummy-in-the-Tummy Venison Pot Pie 64

6822222R1

Made in the USA
Charleston, SC
14 December 2010